LAKAY

A journey of Struggle,
Perseverance, and Hope

David Frederick

Copyright © 2024

All reserved. No part of this book may be reproduced or used in any manner without written permission of the copyright owner except for the use of quotations in a book review.

First Kindle edition July 2024

CONTENTS

Dedication 4

Foreword 6

Introduction 10

    Chapter 1 My Childhood   17

    Chapter 2 The Birthday   25

    Chapter 3 Port-au-Prince   40

    Chapter 4 Bright Lights! Big City   44

    Chapter 5 Trail Of Dreams   48

    Chapter 6 NEVER AGAIN, UN Cholera, A Gift to A Surviving Nation   68

    Chapter 7 The Audacity of FAITH   74

    Chapter 8 Bridging Dreams and Reality: My Year Up Experience   88

    Chapter 9 BLACK IN AMERICA   113

    Chapter 10 Haiti Is Not Dead—Yet   124

    Chapter 11 NEC PLURIBUS IMPAR Haiti, an Experience Like No Other   138

    Chapter 12 Lost in Transit: Stranded Between Worlds   159

    Chapter 13 Leading with Distinction   164

    Conclusion The Country We Ought to Dream For   180

Acknowledgments 187

DEDICATION

DEDICATION

Dear Dahveed, Dawid, and Daud,

When I began writing this book, I hadn't realized that you were the source of every word and the inspiration for the strength that kept me going when discouragement threatened to take hold. Now, as I see Dahveed and Dawid beginning to read and little Daud growing up so fast, I am even more astounded by the unlimited potential each of you possess.

In a few years, I hope that all three of you will be able to read this book for your mother and me, as we sit captivated by the astonishing growth and development you have all experienced. And as you grow older, I pray that you will find this book on a shelf, dust it off, and reflect on how Papi did his best to share the beauty and history of our homeland with you and with the world.

While I am still physically here with you, know that my ears and attention will always be yours, so that I may listen to every word you say. Thank you for making me better and for bringing so much joy and purpose to my life.

With love,

Papi

FOREWORD

Opportunity, Persistence, and Hope

As I was reading David's memoir, there was a line in particular that stuck with me – or two lines, rather, sung by rice farmers in L'Estère: "*S-ou pa travay, mouin p-ape viv / Si-m pa travay, ou p-ape viv.*" In English they sing: "If you don't work, I will not eat / If I don't work, you will not live." The community spirit that lives in those lines, the recognition of our interconnected humanity, shows clearly through David's story. This book is the story of a young man finding and building communities, and his journey – as a young man, as an immigrant, as a community organizer and activist – is courageous. What is inspiring and humbling about his story is perseverance in the face of incredible challenge: from escaping civil unrest in Haiti to coming to America and facing the ordeal of being an undocumented immigrant in this country, David's ability to overcome obstacles in pursuit of his goals is remarkable.

Stories like David's – perseverance in the face of injustices, challenges, and prejudices – are unfortunately common in communities across this country. We live today in a world where talent is distributed evenly while opportunity is not; in a world where the ZIP code a child is born into can predict their future better than any other factor. David's story is set in this world, but it shows what young people can do when given the opportunity to shine. How many young adults could make it from the rice fields of Haiti to Capitol Hill if we gave them a fair shake? How many children in this country would have a brighter future if their mothers and fathers had a path to earn a living wage and support their family?

Seventeen years ago, I founded an organization called Year Up to provide that opportunity for low-income young adults. Its mission was simple: to provide young adults with the skills, experience, and support that would empower them to reach their full potential through professional careers and higher education. Since our founding, we have served more than seventeen thousand young adults and provided each one with an opportunity to lift themselves out of poverty and into a livable wage job. I have been given the distinct blessing to lead this organization and to bear witness to some of the most inspiring and courageous journeys, including David's. Through my time working at Year Up, I have been fortunate to see thousands of young adults earn professional careers, buy cars and houses, start and support families, and lead the way towards a brighter future for our communities. What all these young adults share – what you can clearly see in David's story – is the overwhelming power of persistence. In the words of Calvin Coolidge:

"Nothing in the world can take the place of Persistence. Talent will not; nothing is more common than unsuccessful men with talent. Genius will not; unrewarded genius is almost a proverb. Education will not; the world is full of educated derelicts. Persistence and determination alone are omnipotent. The slogan 'Press On' has always solved and always will solve the problems of the human race."

I have always loved that quote, and believe resolutely that one can achieve anything if they are willing to work hard and pay the price.

Through my work at Year Up and through reading David's story, I have learned about the power of hope. Hope is that great beam of light that shines so bright it penetrates your being. It is an unstoppable force, it has great power, and I see it in the lives of our young adults each day. There is nothing that gives me more belief in our journey than when I have the chance to look in the hopeful eyes of Year Up students. I see the future of our society in those eyes and I believe fervently that our generation's greatest opportunity is to ensure that we never darken that beam of hopeful light. Hope must never become hopelessness.

David's memoir ends with the conclusion "The Country We Ought to Dream For." While it focuses on how Haiti can move beyond its issues with its economic and political systems, it caused me to reflect on the country we as Americans ought to dream for. I believe we ought to dream for a country where every young adult has the opportunity to reach their full potential. We ought to dream for a country with true equality, free from the structures of racism and oppression that currently hold power in our society. We ought to dream for a country where we take in and shelter the tired, the poor, and the huddled masses. We ought to dream, and make our country one that lives up to its promise of opportunity for all.

David's story is one of opportunity, persistence, and hope – three things which are desperately needed in our country today. I am glad, though, that we have young adults like David working to build a brighter future. When you hear his story, you just know he is going to do something amazing to change the world. In fact, you don't even doubt it.

Gerald Chertavian

Founder and Former CEO, Year Up

INTRODUCTION

INTRODUCTION

When I set out on the journey of writing "Lakay," I was an undocumented immigrant, grappling with a tangled web of fears and hopes, dreams and realities. Today, as I re-release "Lakay", I do so as a U.S. citizen. To be frank, I have always wanted to write a book for as long as I can remember; however, I did not expect the process to be both therapeutic and rewarding at the same time. I did not expect that, in doing so, I would discover apart of me I was not aware of even existed; I did not expect to rediscover my path. A path that began so far from where I am now, and one that leads far into the future.

I look back on the process of penning this book as both a voyage of self-discovery and a testament to the transformative power of perseverance. While my personal circumstances have changed, the situation in my homeland of Haiti has, sadly, continued to deteriorate.

In the six years since I first published *Lakay*, Haiti has been ensnared in a relentless grip of turmoil and violence. The once vibrant streets of Port-au-Prince are now overrun with more than two hundred gangs. Kidnappings and massacres are rampant. The brazen assassination of President Jovenel Moïse at his residence marked a gruesome chapter in our history. Overdue elections have caused the House and Senate to shutter, claiming the destabilization of a crucial institutions. Powerful gangs have even briefly taken over the Palais of Justice, which has further eroded the fabric of our society.

Yet, in the face of these seemingly insurmountable challenges, I see flickers of hope. The resilience and resistance that has long defined us as a nation is now more palpable than ever, and manifests in a rising tide of change led by a new generation of Haitians, both at home and throughout the diaspora. I see a burgeoning movement that transcends religious beliefs and political affiliations, united in its singular aim to uplift our land.

This movement is epitomized by the collective endeavor of farmers who have banded together to build a canal, thereby ensuring the irrigation of their lands. To me, this is emblematic of the people becoming the very change agents they have long awaited. Rather than remaining passive recipients of help, they are taking matters into their own hands, acting as the architects of their own destiny.

Just as the water from the canal will nourish the land, this movement has planted a powerful seed in the fertile soil of our nation's spirit. The burgeoning tree of the KPK movement, born from this seed, is boundless in its potential. Its branches stretch far and wide, reaching even the remote corners of the Northeast, where people have heeded the call to shape their own futures and take steps toward irrigating their lands.

In writing this book, I was reminded of Toussaint Louverture's last words after he had been captured by the French. He so famously said, "In overthrowing me, they have uprooted the trunk of liberty of the blacks; it will grow back because its roots are many and deep."

It has never been in our DNA to accept what others have repeatedly and consistently told us. For more than two hundred years now, it has been like an unwanted nightmare to be told that democracy is not for us Haitians, that a prosperous country is out of our reach, or that our land has been poisoned, making it impossible to produce the fruit of liberty. However, I have come to know and believe one thing: our spirit has always imagined greater possibilities.

We have always faced even the worst situations head on, no matter the cost. At Haiti's core is the slogan "Freedom or Death." We know and remember how our story began, and what the end result was. At the height of the most brutal and most prosperous slave trade where more slaves were dying than being born, mothers killed their own children rather than allow them grow up enslaved on the plantation. Through it all, we have dared to d seek a greater possibility—one where freedom, equality, and autonomy are the cornerstone of society. Our forefathers' determination was not just a dream, for it gave birth to the first black country and the first and only successful slave rebellion. Like a phoenix, a new nation was born out of nothing than its very own ashes.

More than two centuries later, in the midst of what seems to be hopelessness, let history be a reminder of what greater possibility can push us to achieve. Our resilience, determination, and perseverance gave birth to the blue and red flag, a flag to represent freedom and equality. In the center of the flag is the coat of arms featuring a cannon and pikes surrounding a palm tree—a testament to liberation from enslavement that recalled the "liberty trees" planted during the French and American revolutions. The palm tree was surmounted by a Phrygian cap, the little floppy red hat originally worn by slaves in ancient Rome that was used by sans-culottes during the French Revolution to show their readiness to upend the social order.[1]

At that critical time in history, conflicts between slaves and their masters ended the same way every time. Slaves were beaten, sometimes to death, and the ruler of the plantation once again deterred an uprising on his land. However, our forefathers flipped the script by not only beating the Spanish and English, but the French as well, including the most feared General Napoleon Bonaparte. In doing so, we sent a

---

1   Laurent Dubois, Haiti: The Aftershocks of History (New York: Henry Holt and Company, LLC 2012), 58.

message that rang loud and clear in every slave's ear around the globe and planted the seed of freedom in the heart of the most cautious slaves, offering them a taste of hope they only dared to experience through dreams. Our story told them freedom was possible, and liberty was within their reach. That is what greater possibilities can give birth to—an outcome that is beyond us and can reshuffle history and how people see and perceive **BLACK PEOPLE**.

When I finally set my mind to write this book, I was faced with two important questions. The first question was, *What happened to my community?*

This book traces my own journey from *LAKAY* (home), which runs through Saint-Marc, Haiti, where I grew up and first learned the power of a persevering and optimistic spirit. I discuss how we as people can exhibit both the best of human nature and the worst of it. While part of this book includes my recollections of the environment, people, and important events in history and how they have impacted Haiti now, this is not a full-blown memoir. These recollections are simply to explain my frame of thinking and what was happening from my viewpoint at that moment in time. Therefore, it is not a history book and should not be treated as such. The events and conversations discussed are described as I remember them or as remembered by those people I spoke to.

Someone who grew up in Haiti may be able to vividly remember these memories, and those who were not born in the land would be able to envision themselves moving along the road I have traveled because, at the end of the day, we have all traveled on that road. We might not come from the same place or end up at the same destination, but at one point in time we have all shared those moments.

INTRODUCTION

The second question that kept entertaining my spirit was, *How do I inspire my readers to persevere in overcoming obstacles while still holding to hope?* While in this part of the book some of the chapters are connected to the previous ones, most of them are supposed to be read as standalone chapters that contain the lessons I have learned at that time. This part of the book is mostly a call to action. It reminds us of who we truly are, and how we can use obstacles to push forward. I attempt to offer some brief ideas on how I believe we can proceed.

While it is true that Haiti's current problems are urgent and critical, I surely do not believe they are impossible to overcome. Throughout my visit in the local markets, the rural side of Haiti, meeting students and entrepreneurs, I can say without a doubt the future of the country is bright—as long as my beloved countrymen and countrywomen can find the common ground to work together. The untapped potential I see is incredible, just as it was more than two centuries ago.

And so, I invite you to join me on this journey— and encourage you to bring a family member or friend along as well. Create a circle. Impactors like to be in the company of like-minded individuals who are committed to being positive change agents for Haiti. It is my hope that this book can at the very least ignite a more favorable discourse around our country, and, in doing so, help to bring about the positive change that is long overdue. For Haiti is very much alive – it lives within each and every one of us.

LAKAY

Chapter 1
MY CHILDHOOD

Ever since I was a little boy, I've been told that I am a dreamer. Time would reveal the truth of that characterization. Now, when I close my eyes, I can trace my evolution—from the boy others doubted to the man many admire. From the scrawny child with an oversized head filled with big dreams, to the robust man who grew to fit those dreams and that head. Driven by a heart full of ambition, I envisaged the inception of my dream in a nation vastly different from the one I find myself in now. As I reminisce about those formative years, I invite you to accompany me on this road paved with my thoughts and experiences reflected in these pages.

My dream begins in a different voice. My dream begins in my mother tongue, Haitian Creole. She molded me into the expressive man that I am today; guiding the rhythm and direction of my thoughts. It's the language I employ to convey my deepest emotions to my wife; the melodic phrases with which I use to caress her:

> *Cheri dous, mwen anvi w' tankou tè sèk k'ap tan lapli. Mwen vle souse w' tankou jan moun souse myèl. Le w tonbe sou janm mwen, ou fè tout san'm koule tankou rivyè dlo k'ap soti sou yon mon. bel negès, men mwen. Pran m', kouri avè m', fè m' pèdi tout bon sans mwen, fè m' bliye si m sou tè oubyen anlè. Touche m', manye m', karese m', jiskaske Sen Espri pran mwen epi m' tonbe pale tout lang.*

Yet how my mother tongue can be cruelly striking to anyone who crosses me. She can be one emotion, and yet she encompasses all emotions. The spirit of the language itself longs to be independent. Some of its most famous sayings are so difficult to properly translate that even a language specialist with a degree from Harvard would not be able to translate these sayings belonging to Haitian Creole alone.

MY CHILDHOOD

In these times, she is selfish without the desire to share her beauty with people outside her culture.

It was in Haiti where I was born and where I grew up. My home is there: Saint-Marc, Haiti. I have lived in many other places, Port-au-Prince, Haiti, and Miami, Florida, but Saint-Marc defines me. It is the very loud sound of the fat roosters too lazy to walk to another neighborhood to welcome the new day, the sound of the students gossiping and giggling waking up early to go to school as their mothers yell at them in Creole telling them to hurry, the loud voices of the merchants passing by. The lingering smells of the fried pork with banana, what we Haitians know as "griot," the moto taxis driving right past your feet as fast and worry-free as a gazelle, as dangerous as a missile. When I see these images, Mwen konnen mwen LAKAY: I know I am HOME.

I often liken my native language to my mother, as I was nurtured in her embrace and she in mine. Haitian Creole resonates in my psyche, its presence steadfast and indomitable. It's an intrinsic part of my identity.

My family's home stood atop a hill in Lascirie, a place renowned for "morne Calvaire." On Good Friday, devotees would ascend from across the country, bearing candles and adorned in pristine white , hoping to transfer their burdens to the "Saints" in exchange for good fortune and joy. To truly grasp my essence, one must first understand my origins. Every person has a narrative, and every tale starts somewhere. Mine begins in Lascirie.

As a boy, joy came easily, even though we had little. My father was the more stringent parent. When our antics exhausted my mother's patience, she'd hand us over to him, and his reprimands were unequivocal. Anything nearby could serve as an instrument of discipline – a belt, igwaz (a whip fashioned from knotted beef skin), an electrical cord, even clothing hangers. Yet, his boundless love for us was unmistakable. He was convinced that any chastisement he gave us would be kinder than society's penalties, or the disgrace an ill-informed choice might impose on the family legacy they had so painstakingly built.

The small canal near my house would mirror my joy anytime I passed it. I vividly recall the morning cries of merchants exclaiming, "Labapen boulli, labapen boulli!" (boiled chestnut! Boiled chestnut!) I can remember the sweet scent of the akasan (Haitian cornmeal) that would wake me up, and how I always looked forward to drinking some.

Augustin and Zilema, two seniors who lived opposite us, hold a special place in my memories. They maintained two vast properties with backyards brimming with coconut trees, blood-red apples that tasted even sweeter than honey, sun-yellow mangoes, and the juiciest almonds. We, the neighborhood children, would stealthily enter their property seeking something to eat, but woe unto us if Augustin caught us. To outwit him, one of us would scout from the front while the rest sneaked in from the back. Passing by Augustin's place, we'd hear his muttering, "Here come the little thieves." I was left puzzled as to how a person in his late sixties or early seventies could have thrown rocks so hard, and with such accuracy.

When it was the season to harvest the apples, we all tried to get on his good side just to receive an invitation to pick apples. Sometimes it worked, and sometimes he saw right through our deception and cursed at us. However, because we lived nearby, Augustin never stayed angry at us for too long. Something could have happened yesterday, but the very next day, he would call my mom to get water from his well for free. The way I grew up was a blessing. Everyone was close, and we sincerely felt like family.

On Saturdays, our neighbors Mrs. Pierre-Eddy and her two kids Peter and Edwin would attend the service at their church and then come straight home. Sometimes, Peter and Edwin would stay by the window and watch us play outside. However, they would never dare to come out because if they did, Mrs. Pierre-Eddy would discipline them. There was also Pharel. He was a shy, lanky kid who lived two houses down from us, who always tried his best to stay out of trouble.

He was not allowed to play with us because his mom considered us to be naughty, and she did not want us to corrupt him. Yet, it was clear to see that he wanted to play with us very badly. Sunday was our church day, and we usually woke up early so that we could be on time for the weekly service, especially because we had to walk about three or four miles to get there.

Every year, we awaited January 2. On that day, we would all meet at École Frère Hervé, a Catholic elementary and middle school, for an annual festival known as "Kèrmès." For me, the best part of Kèrmès was the anticipation.for. Because the event was one of the biggest activities in the city, everyone was expected to wear their very best attire. My mom would buy our clothes from the neighboring city of Port-au-Prince so that we would not have to wear the same clothing as the other kids in the area. However, sometimes my mom would get her check late and would not have time to travel outside our city to buy the clothes. My older sister, Samuella, would pick up the check and cash it at the local Socabank. On those days, my mom went to the market looking for merchants who came from Panama and Curacao. These merchants sold clothing that was not very popular in the city. Once she finally made the purchases, the excitement of wearing new clothing would consume my thoughts; at night, I would dream of wearing the clothes. Sometimes, if my mom bought the clothes on December 31, I would try to persuade my parents to allow me to wear the clothes early to no avail.

We would go to the Kèrmès a bit later in the evening to ensure that people would notice us as we made an entrance. By the time we arrived, most of the people would be in groups. Students from the all-girls school would be on one side, while students from the all-boys school would be on another. Students from the lower schools would be in a different section. Students who spoke French would try to be in the same group as well. Games would be everywhere. There would be raffles, soccer matches, shooting guns, and basketball games.

After the Kèrmès, everyone would head to the "MASIFE." This was a pole filled with car oil. At the very top of it was a prize. Whoever could climb to the top of the pole would receive the prize. Most people would fail many times before one person would actually climb high enough to reach the prize. Some people would put ashes on themselves to have an edge, but even then, it was not easy. To finish the day, almost everyone would go to Mingo Studio & Video to take pictures. If a person did not go to the Kèrmès the next day everyone would know, because the person would not be wearing good clothes.

During the summer, there were three big activities: soccer, shooting marbles, and swimming in the nearby river. Our soccer team's name was *Papè Chay*, which means one who is not afraid of adversity. Indeed, the team was not intimidated by anything or anyone. Any championship that we were a part of, we won; therefore, on every occasion we picked up more supporters, constantly inspiring fear in the opposing teams.

When it came to shooting marbles, we had five players who were known for being the best: Woody, Gordon, Edner, Neckson, and my sister, Keren. There was no chance to win when playing against any of them. As long as they had marbles with them and you were playing, you could lose.

Another game, often played by the girls while we were shooting marbles, was ossicle, also known as knucklebones. An "osselet" is often played with the small bones from the ankles of sheep or goats, though in modern times, they're frequently replaced with small, similarly shaped objects made of metal, wood, or plastic. The traditional version of the game includes five small pieces, with one being distinct, often in color or size. This distinct piece is sometimes called the "jack" or "key" piece. The basic premise of the game involves throwing and catching these pieces in various sequences.

In the first round, the players picked up all four ossicles, one at a time. In the second round, they would pick up two ossicles at a time, then three, at a time, and finally, all four at once.

At night, we would all reconvene under the light pole to play hide and seek, crack jokes, and share riddles.

In Saint-Marc, roads were not just for transportation: roads were where friends and families walked harmoniously. They were where we shared our thoughts and built relationships. At night, they were where we played. The roads were also where we studied for exams and did our homework. I have many fond memories of Saint-Marc. But like anything in life, all those things that I grew up enjoying in life had to come to an end. I must admit that I did not see the end coming.

Chapter 2
THE BIRTHDAY

The roar of a vast crowd filled the expansive conference hall. Campaigners waved vibrant papers, each emblazoned with the face of their chosen candidate. Election fervor had gripped Haiti. The 1990 Haitian presidential elections were unpredictable from the onset. Among the eleven candidates greenlit by the Provisional Electoral Council (CEP) to vie for the presidency, two began to stand out as popular favorites. Mark Bazin, a World Bank veteran and ex-finance minister under Jean Claude Duvalier's tainted regime, had made efforts to combat corruption, albeit with limited success. Contesting against Bazin was Jean-Bertrand Aristide, a novice in the political arena.

Aristide was known as a short, frail, and plain-looking man. He wore large round glasses, reminiscent in thickness to the glass bottle of Kola champagne. Affectionately nicknamed "Titid," a moniker more suitable for a child, he was destined to become a prominent figure on the global stage. With a skin tone echoing the dark-roasted beans offered by coffee merchants in the shanties of his home region, Port-Salut, he resonated deeply with the disenfranchised majority of Haiti (Nicholls, 2011).

The political charm of Aristide stemmed from his remarkable courage and spellbinding oratory prowess. He was recognized as the priest and radio preacher who boldly voiced dissent against Baby Doc before 1986 and continued opposing remnants of the Duvalierist regime thereafter (Hallward, 2007).

His congregation cherished his nuanced political references, savored his keen wit, echoed his words like cherished scripture, engaged with his insightful queries, and responded emotionally on cue. Their affection for the diminutive Titid mirrored the Haitian spirit—

both appeared small and fragile, yet both possessed the audacity to challenge dominating forces (Wilentz, 2001).

Before 1988, few outside Haiti were familiar with Aristide. His rise in politics, intertwined with grassroots radio shows, telediol (rumors), and sermons, largely escaped the international lens. Yet, by the late 20th century, as he established himself among Haiti's most influential leaders, foreign diplomats scurried for insights into the populist priest's background (Dupuy, 2007).

Aristide's sermons, rich in Creole idioms, struck potent chords against the Tonton Macoutes and even the United States. This fearsome militia, dubbed the "TonTon Macoutes," took its name from Creole lore about an "uncle" figure who abducted and punished wayward children, sealing them in sacks to later consume them (Abbott, 1991). Consequently, these tormentors became objects of terror, not just for children but for the entire nation. Businesspeople and political adversaries hesitated before opposing them, wary of their demands for hefty bribes (Diederich & Burt, 2005).

Aristide's leftist economic views resonated deeply with the majority of Haiti's urban poor. Contrary to the belief of many, Aristide's movement didn't emerge out of thin air. Throughout Haiti, he garnered steadfast support, notably from the ti legliz (small churches). Within these churches, fervent priests galvanized their congregations, supporting various candidates. Before Aristide, no politician had tapped into this influential segment of both the young and old. Historically, Haiti experienced a stark divide: a large segment of marginalized rural peasants and a minority of urban dwellers (Wilentz, 2001).

The agricultural crisis during the 1970s and 80s forced peasants off their lands. These unemployed individuals, often living just a few miles from the capital, yearned for leadership. They sought someone to transform their dormant political potential into tangible power. Jean Bertrand Aristide was the sole figure who rose to this challenge (Dupuy, 2007).

By October's end, after previously showing reluctance towards presidential aspirations, Aristide emerged as the presidential nominee for FNCD (National Front for Democratic Convergence). This decision was significantly influenced by Roger Lafontant, the former Duvalier Interior Minister, announcing his candidacy. "Bloke Makout Yo" became Aristide's rallying cry. Despite the lack of reliable polling data to confirm his popularity, enormous voter registrations occurred when Aristide announced his candidacy. The audacious courage Aristide displayed during Baby Doc's reign became a pivotal element of his political identity. Furthermore, voters were enchanted by Aristide's knack for weaving indigenous Haitian cultural symbols into his electrifying speeches.

He named his movement "Lavalas", the Creole term for flash flood. Just as torrential rains would wash away debris, Aristide promised to cleanse Haiti of its deep-rooted corruption (Hallward, 2007). He also employed agricultural vernacular, such as rache manyonk (evacuate the manioc) and dechoukaj (to uproot), symbolizing the need to overhaul the political landscape. Recognizing that many of his supporters were illiterate, Aristide chose the rooster, revered in Haitian culture for its roles in Voodoo rituals and cockfights, as his campaign emblem.

Despite facing daunting challenges, including a grenade attack in downtown Port-au-Prince just two weeks before the election, nothing could deter the Lavalas movement's momentum. Aristide, with his idealism, youth, and charisma, symbolized a fresh start for many

Haitians yearning to break free from past dictatorships. Remarkably, on December 16, 1990, Haiti witnessed an unprecedented democratic and peaceful presidential election. On election day, even without the anticipated oversight of U.S. diplomats who had predicted a Bazin win, Haitians, particularly in impoverished Aristide strongholds, queued up as early as dawn. Eager to ink their thumbs beside the rooster symbol, some polling station lines stretched for miles. Many stations remained understaffed well into the afternoon due to widespread disorganization (Nicholls, 2011).

A day after the voting concluded, the electoral commission unveiled preliminary results, indicating that Aristide had secured an uncontestable majority, eliminating the need for a runoff election. The conclusive count released on December 23 positioned Aristide at the forefront with a remarkable 67.48% (Smith, 2001). Upon his victorious declaration, Aristide extended an apology to American observers for any perceived exaggeration in his conduct during the election. However, the atmosphere remained tense. U.S. Ambassador Alvin P. Adams, in a cautionary tone, recited the Creole adage, "Apre bal, tanbou lou" — after the festivity, the weight of the drums is felt — reminding Aristide of imminent challenges (Farmer, 1994).

The nation basked in joyous celebration. Aristide, with his eloquent speeches and innate political prowess, embodied the hopes and aspirations of many. He was viewed as the long-awaited beacon of change — the leader who stood firm on ideals and education. Yet, the global community observed with a cautious eye, particularly due to Aristide's left-leaning and populist inclinations. Despite these reservations, they largely supported Haiti's democratic venture. It seemed Haiti was steering towards a democratic renaissance (Bell, 2001).

In a country historically dominated by mulatto leadership, Aristide, a black president, stood out. Contrasted against the wealthy decision-makers of the nation, he was a man of modest means. Fluent in both Creole, his mother tongue, and French, he often seemed an outsider in corridors of power. The elites, skeptical of his capabilities and loyalty, deemed him an ill-fit to helm their nation. Tragically, by the close of his inaugural year in office, Aristide's presidency was brutally interrupted by a military coup in September 1991 (Wilentz, 1990).

The Return of the White Dove

It took three years of relentless efforts, both domestically and on an international scale, to witness the almost unimaginable. A parallel could be drawn to 1973, when Argentina's Juan Perón reclaimed the presidency after a coup d'état (Page, 1983). The world waited with bated breath, curious about the unfolding future.

Community groups across Haiti had poured their energy into rejuvenating their surroundings. Streets shone with cleanliness, devoid of any litter. Enthusiastic residents with brooms and shovels cleared heaps of trash. Buildings adorned fresh coats of paint, and the ubiquitous image of "Titid" and the symbolic rooster of Aristide's movement decorated every nook and cranny. The air was thick with hope as many passionately sang, "Menl anle-a, l'ap vini" (Look to the sky, he's returning).

As thousands converged in Port-au-Prince in eager anticipation, a collective cheer erupted island-wide upon hearing of Aristide's return after a three-year U.S exile. Embraces and handshakes were exchanged, and cries of "koukou ekou," reminiscent of the emblematic rooster, resonated. It symbolized freedom and hope. Eduis Bathold, a 29-year-old who stood behind the barriers set by the U.S. Army, captured the sentiment: "Before, we slept with one eye open; now we rest peacefully. Once starved, we now feel nourished" (Dupuy, 2007).

In a symbolic gesture before addressing the nation, Aristide released a white dove, emphatically declaring the promise of security at all times. He radiated optimism in his inaugural address, stating, "Today marks the dawn of an unwavering democracy. The vigilant eyes of justice remain open, and security will be unwavering."

However, the trajectory of Aristide's leadership took a turn no one could foresee. He transformed, mirroring the very oppression he once vehemently opposed.

My parents often reminisced about the reigns of terror under Papa Doc (François Duvalier) and Baby Doc (Jean-Claude Duvalier). These dictators had ears everywhere; informants on each street corner (Abbott, 2011). A mere whisper of dissent could lead to unspeakable punishment — fifty-two brutal lashings. Those who dared to openly challenge the regime would disappear into oblivion, with their families too petrified to question their fate.

The Precursors

Your recounting of the events in Saint-Marc provides an intense firsthand account of the political unrest and upheaval that was taking place in Haiti during that period. The vivid descriptions bring the reader into the thick of the action and underscore the dangers of political activism in such volatile times.

The narrative seems personal, raw, and historically accurate, detailing the stakes and the palpable tension that was felt by those on the ground. This personal perspective offers an invaluable lens into the complexities of the situation.

I've taken the liberty to provide a revised version that amplifies the imagery, streamlines the narrative, and clarifies certain elements:

In the pivotal span from late 2003 to early 2004, Saint-Marc's traditional festivities hung in precarious balance due to tumultuous political undercurrents. Two key factions held sway. Ramicost—the Rassemblement des Militants Consequents de la Commune de St. Marc, an expansive civilian opposition rooted in the Lascierie sector— demanded President Aristide's resignation. Conversely, the ardently pro-Aristide Bale Wouze, led by the fiery and democratically detached Deputy Amanus Mayette, sought to cement Saint-Marc's loyalty to the regime. Despite their government connections, their imperious conduct rendered them widely unpopular.

By 2003, opposition strength swelled as the state either tacitly allowed or outright sponsored brutal suppressions, often enacted by police, gangs, or the notorious chimères. The chilling discoveries of abducted journalists' desecrated bodies, or the menacing threats to imprisoned opponents, added to the simmering discord.

Nestled in Lascirie, I found myself ensconced with Ramicost, frequently attending their passionate assemblies. The atmosphere palpably shifted on February 5, 2004. In Gonaives, ex-military forces ousted the police and asserted their intent to dethrone Aristide. Mirroring this defiance, Saint-Marc's Ramicost galvanized an immense gathering. Reports detailed the storming of the police station, street barricades, frenzied lootings, and two lamentable fatalities.

In a heady blend of curiosity and solidarity, I once joined a Ramicost rally, recorder in hand, immersing myself in their fervor.

Our jubilant chants resurrected anthems that had once condemned the Duvaliers, symbolizing the cyclical nature of power and tyranny. In a bold challenge, we dared approach Bale Wouze's stronghold, only to be met with stifling tear gas and disorienting gunshots.

My venture earned a frantic reprimand from my mother. I tried rationalizing, pointing out my father's similar endeavors with CNEH (Confédération National des Enseignats d'Haiti) in Port-au-Prince. He too resisted the regime, echoing the frustrations of many teachers left unpaid or unacknowledged.

However, tensions in Saint-Marc only escalated. The increasingly desolate police force made way for lawless gangs. Emboldened Ramicost members planned a daring rally, a direct march past the opposition. Bale Wouze's response was chillingly lethal. The streets echoed with their malevolent intent, "cleaning" the paths with gunfire. In the midst of the chaos, I found myself desperately evading the very real threat of bullets, the harrowing sounds piercingly close.

In the shadow of 2003's political unrest, Saint-Marc's streets were no longer ours. The stark division between Ramicost and Bale Wouze was glaringly evident, a silent thunderstorm was waiting to break.

During one of the protests, the chaos escalated beyond belief. Friends were injured, gunshots punctuated the air, and fear wrapped its cold fingers around us all. The dark omens didn't escape anyone, especially when Prime Minister Yvon Neptune arrived. The very skies seemed to react to his presence, turning tumultuous and foreboding.

It was my mother, with her intrinsic maternal foresight, who sensed the impending danger. Close to Ramicost's headquarters and given my father's ties to the opposition, our home was no longer a safe haven. Heeding her intuition, we abandoned our abode in Lascirie, seeking temporary refuge in Blockoss.

By dawn, Saint-Marc was a city on the run. Everywhere, there were echoes of desperation—a frenzied rush to escape the mounting tension. At the bus station, the atmosphere was thick with anxiety, with families clutching at each other, seeking the shared warmth of familiar faces, waiting to see what would happen next.

My mother was our anchor. Holding my brother and me close, she navigated through the pressing crowd. Salvation came in the form of a familiar face, the son of one of my mother's students. Suddenly, the pressing weight of the crowd eased as we were ushered onto a bus.

As we moved farther from Saint-Marc, the scenes unfolding outside painted a grim picture. Desperation, fights, fear—Saint-Marc was changing, and not for the better. Each mile that widened the gap between us and the city was a cruel reminder that home, as we knew it, might never be the same. I was tormented by questions about our neighbors and friends. Would Augustin and Zilema, those aged stalwarts of Lascirie, withstand this storm?

With each turning of the bus wheels, my heart grew heavier. The streets, the voices, the memories—they all seemed to blur into a distant past. I yearned for the familiar comforts, for peace, for reconciliation. But as the city's skyline faded in the distance, the looming dread became more palpable. Saint-Marc, the place I held so dear, was now the epicenter of my deepest fears.

The Day

For many survivors of such massacres, recalling the very day everything unraveled can be harrowing. Even after a decade, some victims' families tremble at the thought of sharing their heart-wrenching tales. Though many summon the courage to speak, their stories are often interspersed with tears, the weight of their memories inducing haunting nightmares.

I chose to document this grim chapter of my life in this book as a way to find closure, and also as a stark reminder of one of the most devastating events the city of Saint-Marc has ever witnessed. The inherent safety we once felt, the smiles that adorned our faces, the carefree nights – all seemed a distant memory. On that fateful day, an insidious evil lurked on our doorsteps, annihilating the innocence that our beloved city once basked in.

On February 11, 2004, a mere day after we fled the city, the morning news reported that Bale Wouze had overrun Lascirie, setting aflame the houses of Ramicost leaders and many others in the vicinity. Lascirie's central rallying point was consumed in fire.

The broadcast showed plumes of smoke billowing as homes succumbed to the flames. My thoughts raced, grappling with the tragic reality unfolding before my eyes. Had our collective legacy become this? A tale of overpowering the meek with violence, instilling fear through brutality, and erasing memories to absolve oneself of wicked deeds? I staunchly refused to believe that this was the pinnacle of our existence.

In retrospect, this day indelibly marked one of the bloodiest chapters in Saint-Marc's history.

Given my absence during these events, I reached out to friends and other survivors to piece together the occurrences of that day. Their recollections painted a bleak picture: a frenzied exodus to the mountains, fleeing the relentless gunshots; a desperate race against time, marked by fallen comrades and silent prayers.

The gravity of the crimes committed on that ominous day was so profound that many survivors, overwhelmed by trauma, suppressed their memories.

The assigned prosecutor documented several heinous acts from February 11:

- *Two young women, Anne (34 years old) and Kétia (22 years old), searching for their boyfriends who were kidnapped and killed during the massacre, were raped on the floor of the police station in Saint-Marc by members of "Balé Wouzé."*

- *Three adolescents captured by members of "Balé Wouzé" were tied with a rope and thrown alive from the helicopter into the sea at Amaniy-Les Bains; their bodies were found.*

- *Two people in the helicopter were decapitated and their bodies were thrown out into thin air.*

- *The octogenarian Luc Paultre was seriously burned during the fire on February 12 in his home. The husband of Yvanne Clairvoyant, who had just delivered a baby 15 days earlier, was decapitated with an axe and thrown into a fire.*

- *Nickson François was tied to a pickup truck and dragged across town.*

The grim aftermath of such a horrifying event is one that lingers, deeply imprinted in the memories of those who witnessed it and those who suffered the most. Bodies charred beyond recognition, or worse, dismembered and scattered, bore a chilling testament to the barbaric acts committed that day. No sacredness of life was acknowledged, no respect for the dead remained; many were denied the dignity of a proper burial.

A particularly haunting account emerges from the chaos. Somoza, Vickès, Ti Jean Claude, Ernst Pascal, Biron, Amanus, and Armstrong — all prominent members of Bale Wouze — forcibly entered Pastor Daméus Anulaire's home. One heart-wrenching account that remains indelibly marked in the collective memory is that of Kénol St-Gilles. He was violently seized from under a bed, where he had sought refuge after a gunshot wound, only to be thrown alive into flames. And all this horror unfolded before his mother's very eyes, a trauma unimaginable to most. Such harrowing tales reveal the depths of human cruelty and the lengths to which certain individuals would go to inflict pain and terror on their fellow beings.

The judge's documentation, chilling in its brevity, provides a bleak summary: forty-four dead, some too charred to identify, some vanished without a trace. Twenty-two were identified amidst the remnants of that horrific day. The nature of these deaths, the sheer brutality of the acts, was something never before witnessed. In times past, tyrants might have been content with theft or beatings, but this new breed seemed to derive perverse pleasure not just from killing, but from the excruciating manner of the death itself. They rejoiced in the pain they inflicted and welcomed the air incensed by the smell of the burned human skin accompanied by the agonizing cry of a mother's shattered heart.

Accounts were reported about how one man was taken and thrown inside of a burning house. Sometimes, even when I am trying to envision these events, the justification of an individual throwing another human being into a house on fire is beyond my ability to comprehend. I struggle to comprehend the minds of those who perpetrate such cruelty. What drives a person to throw another into a raging fire? Is mere political affiliation a valid justification for such barbarity? The visceral anguish of the victims' loved ones, the desperate pleas of a mother watching her child perish. The kind of agony she must have felt listening to the voice of someone she had protected for nine months, breastfed for six months, watched grow up right in front of her eyes... now hearing that same cry and unable to do anything. Just pouring out her soul, crying for mercy, but with no one there to help - such scenes are impossible to erase from one's memory. How could they? I will never forget the fear I saw on my mother's face. I cannot forget the sorrow and the pain I saw in many of these families during moments after that day.

I recall Fleurinst's hopeful words from a decade earlier, extolling the virtues of Aristide and the promise of a brighter future. "The country will change so that everybody can find work and food. There should be peace. Aristide will bring peace," said Fleurinst. Like anyone else at that time, that was what we had hoped for. However, the devils of this earth, the ones we Haitians had become too familiar with, did not see us as worthy of such a basic human right and instead they sentenced us to a disheartened hope, a grim reality dominated by malevolent forces, domestic and foreign. The tragedy, in part, stems from the fact that a once-beloved priest, someone entrusted with guiding his flock, could preside over such horrors. His drive to remain in power, it seemed, knew no bounds.

Though time may have moved on and though some perpetrators may no longer be among us, the legacy of that day remains. It's a testament to the insidious nature of unchecked hatred, and the dire consequences it can bring. As a child at that time, it was difficult to comprehend the vastness of this tragedy. Now, as an adult, I find solace in the Holy Spirit, in the belief that even in the face of such immense darkness, there is a guiding force that offers comfort and resilience. But the lessons of that day remain - a sobering reminder of the dangers of unchecked power and the depths to which humanity can sink when driven by hate. When you escape something as heinous as that massacre, when you actually know people who were killed and see how close the scent of death is, an unshakable optimism to see a better Haiti is birthed within your heart. The ramifications of that day were catastrophic. Families were shattered, communities lay in ruins, and the soul of Saint-Marc bore deep wounds. Yet, amid the anguish, tales of resilience emerged – tales of a community that, despite its scars, sought to rebuild, ensuring their history would be remembered and never repeated.

Chapter 3
PORT-AU-PRINCE

Port-au-Prince has its own soundtrack constantly playing in the streets. Port-au-Prince, often referred to as the "City of the People," thrummed with an undeniable energy. As I stepped into its vibrant embrace, the city felt like a living, breathing entity. To the uninitiated, it might just seem like a cacophony of noise. But to those attuned to its rhythms, it was a symphony. The blare of car horns, the chattering of vendors selling their wares, the distant beat of traditional Haitian music — all these sounds melded to create a city that never seemed to sleep.

Streets bustled with commerce and the promise of opportunity. Everywhere I looked, life unfolded in a myriad of colors and emotions. It's no wonder that when asked, many Haitians proudly claim their origins from this pulsating heart of the country. Moreover, for foreigners, saying you were Haitian almost automatically equated to being from Port-au-Prince.

The capital's allure was not just its ceaseless activity. Port-au-Prince was the hub of dreams and aspirations. It housed the majority of our universities, beckoning students from across the nation with the promise of a brighter future. This sentiment resonated deeply within my family tradition. Upon reaching ninth grade, it was customary for us to shift to this city, complete our high school education, and set our sights on higher academic pursuits.

By the time I moved to the capital, much of my family had already relocated to the United States. My father, on the other hand, was engrossed in his Senate campaign in Jeremie. My daily companions in this vibrant and crazy city were my twin brother, Davidson, and our eldest sister, Samuella.

The challenges of city life soon became apparent. On days when my pockets were empty, I'd walk the long 4 to 5 miles to school. The tropical sun would beat down mercilessly, drenching my shirt and causing beads of sweat to form on my forehead. But every drop of sweat, every tired step, was a testament to my resilience and determination. These daily walks were tough, but they were building blocks in the formation of my character. I would often remind myself, especially during the tougher days when hunger gnawed at my stomach, that this phase was temporary, a stepping stone to a brighter future.

In those challenging times, the little things mattered most. A simple cup of water with sugar would keep migraines at bay. When the city plunged into darkness due to power outages, the dim flicker of candles or our family's small gas lamp (lamp tèt gridap) illuminated our nights. During days when funds were tight, and we couldn't refill our lamp with gas, innovation became the key. These experiences instilled a strong belief in me: failure wasn't an option. My parents were giving it their all, and the least I could do was reciprocate their efforts with dedication to my future.

As the days turned into months, I often found solace in a promise my father had made. He'd said that after our high school, Davidson and I would join the family in the United States. The allure of the promised land, with tales of abundant opportunities and even mythical money trees, occupied my thoughts. Some painted America as a land where dreams could be achieved through hard work, where roads opened in every direction and one's destiny was entirely in their own hands. The anticipation of this journey was tinged with exhilaration and a sense of daunting responsibility as I realized that every decision, every path chosen, would be a step I take on my own. As I approached the crossroads, the diverging directions stretched out before me, each one a mystery waiting to be unraveled. I knew every action would shape my future, but the way forward was unclear.

In this melting pot of cultures and dreams, my days in Port-au-Prince were a mosaic of experiences – each day a different shade, each interaction a different hue. From the bustling markets where the air was thick with the aroma of spices and the sounds of church members worshiping nearby the house, to the classrooms where young minds, including mine, were shaped and dreams were kindled, every moment was a brick in the road of my journey. These experiences, both challenging and enriching, were not just passages of time but were the crucibles that molded my identity, my perspectives, and my ambitions.

Chapter 4

BRIGHT LIGHTS! BIG CITY

My eyes had never opened so wide in my entire life. Stepping on American soil for the first time, my senses were engulfed in a whirlwind of unfamiliar sights and sounds. Miami International Airport, with its bustling energy and foreign accents, was unlike anything I had ever experienced. The digital clocks read 7:30 p.m., and the cool, air-conditioned atmosphere sent a shiver down my spine as I realized: It was July 2, 2008, and I was now a Haitian-American.

A medley of emotions—excitement, apprehension, curiosity—washed over me as I eagerly anticipated my first moments outside the airport. Visions of friends who had previously traveled to the U.S. paraded in my mind. They had regaled tales of 12-screen movie theaters, the fast-food delights of McDonald's, and the empowerment of driving their own cars. With their pockets flaunting green dollar bills and handfuls of shiny quarters and dimes, some had returned with an air of superiority, a newfound arrogance that belittled those who hadn't tasted the American dream. Their stories became a distant hum as I entered the car waiting for me outside.

As the vehicle glided along I-95, the city's energy was palpable. Skyscrapers towered above, their windows gleaming under the city lights. Vehicles of all sizes zipped past, their headlights like shooting stars against the twilight. Every element of this new world seemed choreographed, from the orderly traffic to the synchronized stoplights. "So, is this the country that turns people into gold?" I asked myself. My mom, who came to pick me up, was talking to the driver, Brother Orinal, a member of the church my family attended.

"Welcome, brothers!" yelled Orinal, which startled me out of my reverie. "They all look like you, Sister Lavaud, except for his twin. He looks like your husband," he continued to say.

That first night in America, sleep eluded me. The mirror in my modest room became a silent confidant, capturing the reflection of a young man perched on the edge of a grand, uncharted adventure. I whispered to myself, "I am in AMERICA, and I am an AMERICAN… YES! I am HERE," I felt a surge of exhilaration mixed with a tinge of disbelief.

As dawn unfurled its light, it revealed a world that appeared almost otherworldly in its meticulous order. The lawns were like green velvet, perfectly manicured. Cars formed disciplined queues at traffic lights, a synchronized ballet of urban life, contrasting sharply with Haiti's vivacious, controlled chaos. The pristine streets of Miami lacked the boisterous Creole shouts that filled the air back home, the litter-strewn paths, and the ever-present, gritty haze that seemed to hang over everything. Here, life moved with a deliberate purpose and precision that was both awe-inspiring and disorienting.

During weekdays, I observed children – the future leaders of this country – standing patiently on sidewalks, awaiting school buses with a discipline I'd never seen before. Others strolled leisurely to nearby schools, their laughter a carefree melody. I overheard conversations of senior students, deliberating over the vast array of colleges to which they aspired, while some of their peers, nearly invisible beneath the weight of their responsibilities, juggled one or two jobs along with their studies.

During my initial weeks, I felt as if I had been dropped into the midst of New York City's pulsating Fifth Avenue, a place animated with life and incessant motion. I was a still figure amidst the whirlwind, absorbing the orchestrated chaos – the rhythmic footsteps of passersby, the symphony of cars, and the palpable pulse of the city. It dawned on me that while the country might not have literal green money trees, it was abundant with opportunities waiting to be seized or, at the very least, reached for with hopeful hands.

Fast forward a few years, and I found myself addressing an eager group of young professionals at Year Up South Florida. As I shared the lessons I have learned – my roles at AT&T, Nike, Miami Dade College, and my engagement in church – a question emerged from the audience: "How do you manage it all?" I paused, gathering my thoughts. Then, likening my experience to that of a child in a candy store, I explained. Just as a child, long deprived of sweets, would be awestruck in a world brimming with candy, I, too, reveled in every opportunity that America offered. This insatiable hunger for knowledge and experience became my propulsion, my guiding star. In my view, to cease to evolve was akin to letting the fiery flame of purpose flicker and fade.

Chapter 5
TRAIL OF DREAMS

Landing in the United States, I was immediately struck by how politically active citizens were here, particularly young Latinos. In America, these youth seemed like active forces in the political landscape. They were well-versed in political discourse, championing causes like immigration reform and influencing local elections. Their commitment manifested in simple yet impactful actions like make phone calls to representatives or, participate in more audacious demonstrations, such as extensive marches from Miami to Washington, D.C.— each step a testament to their dedication to progressive change

In Haiti, however, the political scene presented a jarring counterpoint. In Haiti the political scene felt stagnant, controlled only by a select few. Citizens often seemed relegated to mere pawns in a grand political chess game, maneuvered and manipulated by the whims of the elite. These leaders, comfortably ensconced away from the fray, often incite their supporters to commit acts of public disturbance and crimes, while they remain unscathed, their names and reputations clean.

For true continuity in governance, Haiti needs a new generation of leaders ready to navigate the nation toward a brighter future. But such a change necessitates a radical shift in the collective psyche of the Haitian people. Moving beyond the role of passive observers, disillusioned by the specter of corruption, it would behoove them to find inspiration in the likes of activist groups in the U.S. like Haitian American Youth of Tomorrow (HAYOT) or Students Working for Equal Rights (S.W.E.R.). Despite recognizing the deep-rooted flaws in the system, these young American activists fiercely advocate for change. They are not content with merely pointing out problems; they bring concrete solutions and innovative strategies to the table, and are part of the conversation.

The fervor found in Haitian protests, though brimming with raw energy, often spirals without direction. Rather than being mere followers in these movements, there's a potential for these individuals to emerge as leaders. The road to such conversion is undoubtedly filled with challenges, but it remains an essential journey for real impact. The power structures in Haiti are insular, rarely opening doors to fresh perspectives or new voices. Those in power are often caught in a self-perpetuating cycle, seldom extending mentorship or guidance to the next generation. This stagnation hinders progress and only further solidifies the power of those who already have it.

But in America, the emphasis on cultivating leadership was unmistakable. In every organization I was a part of, from HAYOT to S.W.E.R., MDC-FIU Wesley, and Minority Students for College Success (M.S.f.C.S.), there was a concerted effort to nurture potential leaders. This ethos of empowerment and growth was something I'd only encountered in my spiritual life during my days at the Tabernacle of Glory, while under the guidance of now-Bishop Gregory Toussaint. In America, I realized,the focus was on empowering individuals, fostering a sense of responsibility, and the importance of contributing positively to the community and society at large.

In the complex mosaic of American politics, immigration remains a contentious and unresolved issue, and is only becoming more so.. This ongoing battle for immigration reform is characterized by a mix of hope and setbacks, reflecting a saga of enduring challenges. Despite significant backing, including support from then-President Bush, the quest for immigration reform faced a severe setback on June 7, 2007.

The Senate voted a disheartening 34 to 61 that marked the failure of a substantial legislative effort. A subsequent attempt, just twenty-one days later, also failed, garnering a vote of 46 to 53.

Amid these setbacks, a new wave of hope surged with the rise of then-Senator Barack Obama in 2008. His candidacy, symbolizing the potential of electing the first Black American President, rekindled aspirations for comprehensive immigration reform. This issue was a fundamental aspect of the then-senator's campaign, imbued with promises of change and progress. Obama's commitment was underscored in his 2008 statement: "I cannot guarantee that it is going to be in the first 100 days. But what I can guarantee is that we will have in the first year an immigration bill that I strongly support and that I'm promoting. And I want to move that forward as quickly as possible."

This era brought a renewed sense of optimism, fostering the belief that, for the first time in many years, a comprehensive approach to immigration reform was attainable. The community envisioned millions of hardworking immigrants stepping out of the shadows, finally recognized and granted rights. However, the this optimism faded by the following year. Despite the president's frequent references to immigration reform in his speeches in 2009 and 2010, there was a noticeable lack of legislative action. No immigration legislation was introduced by the administration in either the Senate or the House, despite having a Democratic majority in both.

On December 15, 2009, then-Democratic Representative Luis Gutierrez of Illinois, who was in office at the time, took a significant step by introducing an immigration bill. This initiative, however, did not garner the necessary backing or public support from the Obama administration, contributing to the series of legislative disappointments in the realm of immigration reform. In the face of these unmet promises and legislative inaction, the community recognized that relying solely on political figures was not enough. This realization led to the birth of the "Trail of Dreams" campaign, a grassroots movement driven by the understanding that true change often requires direct action and consistent advocacy from those most impacted by these policies.

The Trail: Why we walked

In January 2010, four undocumented students—Felipe Matos, Gaby Pacheco, Carlos Roa, and Juan Rodriguez—left Miami to embark on a 1,500-mile journey to our nation's capital. Their goal was to walk and listen to the stories undocumented kids and parents who were too afraid to talk, too scared to share their stories with the world, in every county along their journey. Inspired by their experience having immigrated to the United States at a very young age, they wanted the public to understand they had the same hopes and dreams as American citizens— that they had worked hard to excel in school and contribute to our communities just like them. That "undocumented" should not be such a dirty word, and a barrier towards having a comfortable life here in the States. I, myself, had a similar story. I was undocumented at that time.

Felipe couldn't have put it better when he said, "That decision to walk came from the hopes and dreams and everyday struggles of everyday individuals in Florida, and from the need to overcome the different abuses that we are living in our everyday lives. We are the product of a movement of young people screaming at the top of their lungs and not finding a voice or even a refuge in this nation we have grown to recognize as home."

The students had asked Washington for the following:
- Respect for the rights of workers
- Fulfillment of equal accessibility to education
- Maintaining a just and humane pathway to full citizenship
- Protection of the sacred bonds and unity of our families!

We were all tired of living in the hope that tomorrow would be okay. It was unbearable to think that at any time one could wake up and find out that a loved one had been taken in the dark of night, deported by those who claim to keep our community safe. So we too walked, determined and unafraid. The walk was for us, our family, our friends, and our community.

At the time, I was president of Haitian American Youth of Tomorrow (HAYOT) and a member of the logistics team. I was in charge of facilitating the first day of the journey. I had to make sure everyone from HAYOT had somewhere to meet, eat, and sleep. Our group began our journey in front of the Freedom Tower after a press conference, and made our first stop in North Miami Beach to address the Haitian community. That evening we slept at the Fulford United Methodist Church in North Miami Beach. After a quick debrief, we called it a night.

Early the next day, we began walking again. This time we stopped in Fort Lauderdale; seventeen miles away. Walking such long distances is definitely not easy. I remember how members of our group had already begun complaining about the blisters on their feet. It was only the beginning of what would be a painful journey— not just in terms of the physical pains we were inflicting on ourselves, but also the stories and the struggles we heard along the way.

We walked through the rain, through cold winds. Our shoes were wet, our feet were swollen, and yet we walked. ried to wrap our shoes with tape to give us temporary relief. By the time we got to the meeting place, it was really cold; a few people were waiting for us, and they were all shaking. After we met with the people in the area, we hit the ground again to finish the day. About a dozen people were with us; some gave the walkers clothes and money to continue the journey. Gaby, one of the four walkers, would always say how she cherished those moments. These people gave her and all of us the warmth we needed on that cold day.

The Trail: 2010 Haiti Earthquake Resonance in Distant Land

A few days later, I was back in Miami for classes and was in the HAYOT's office that afternoon. The office, usually a sanctuary of muted sounds and focused diligence, was abruptly pierced by the shrill cry of a breaking news alert. The air seemed to stand still as the announcement cut through the tranquility: "Breaking news! A 7.0 magnitude earthquake has struck Haiti." A frigid shiver snaked down my spine, freezing me in place.

"Not us, not again," I whispered to no one, the words barely escaping my lips as the enormity of the news bore down upon me like a physical weight, pressing against my chest with an almost tangible force.

In that suspended moment, my mind raced to my father and sister, both living at the very heart of the catastrophe. Driven by an urgency that made every second stretch and warp like a rubber band, I hurried home, my thoughts a whirlwind of fear and prayer. Bursting through the door, I blurted out, "Have you heard from Dad and my sister?"

My mother's face, a mirror of my own dread, was etched with lines of worry. "No," she whispered back, her voice trembling like a leaf in the wind, "But we're trying."

The wait that ensued felt like a journey through a desolate landscape of time, each second a mile of anxiety. After three harrowing hours that stretched on like a lifetime, the phone finally rang. They were safe. My father, it seemed, had cheated death in a heart-stopping leap, escaping from our family home mere seconds before it succumbed to the quake's wrath.

While our family grappled with this miraculous reprieve, the broader Haitian community in the United States was undergoing a seismic shift. In the earthquake's aftermath, Janet Napolitano, then Secretary of Homeland Security, announced the "Temporary Protected Status" (TPS) for Haitian nationals residing in the US. This declaration was a beacon of hope, a rare respite from the ominous cloud of deportation that had long loomed over many of us.

Yet, as I soaked in the solace of this reprieve, a bitter cocktail of guilt and anger simmered within me. This wasn't the first calamity to ravage my homeland. Only two years prior, a quartet of hurricanes had unleashed their fury on Haiti, leaving a trail of destruction in their wake. Then, our pleas for protective status had echoed unanswered. Now, with the earthquake's devastation impossible to ignore, claiming over 100,000 souls, the US government extended its hand of mercy. This belated gesture gnawed at my heart, evoking a soul-searching question: "Why did it take another immense loss for our plight to be acknowledged?

The Trail: The stories

A few days after my college final exam, I found myself traveling back to rejoin the walkers. I met them around Daytona, Florida. Among the many stories people shared on the trail, one that lingers vividly in my memory is that of Oscar, a perceptive fifth grader. Felipe spoke about fellow walker Oscar's aspiration to become a therapist. His young mind, already burdened with understanding the labyrinthine complexities of his reality, shone with a precocious intelligence. What struck Felipe the most wasn't just Oscar's clarity of thought, but his courage in vocalizing his struggle. When the moment came for Oscar to address a crowd during a press conference, he stood with an unwavering resolve wiser than his tender age. His words pierced the air, a heartfelt plea to then-president Obama: "Please, give my parents a chance. It would be too painful to lose them." This eleven-year-old, thrust into a world where innocence is a luxury, struggled to make sense of a life where his sister faced derogatory slurs at school, his father teetered on the brink of deportation, and his mother's talents were confined to the limited realm of cake decoration. In his quest to find comfort, Oscar turned to history books, seeking refuge in their pages, a balm for his wounded young soul.

Oscar's story awakened memories of walker Juan's poignant reflections. As we continued walking, Juan's voice, tinged with desperation and resolve, broke the silence: "How much longer are we truly willing to wait? I've been haunted by nightmares of an officer handcuffing a loved one and coldly declaring, "I am going to deport this person tomorrow. Will you wait another six months for Congress to talk about immigration reform?" This isn't just a fear; it's our reality, a recurring agony. And yet, we delude ourselves into believing that patience is our only recourse. How many more souls must we lose? WHO are you prepared to sacrifice next? Could it be me? Perhaps you? Or will it remain a distant concern as long as it's someone else in a place you've never been? Is our complacency justified, so long as the shadow of loss doesn't darken our doorstep? Why must the safety of our loved ones hinge on the whims of those driven by greed or the hunger for re-election? Can we, in good conscience, claim they represent our interests, our voices? I am but a youth, armed with a sea of questions and a heart yearning for answers...

These events occurred thirteen years ago. I am asking you the same questions today. What's your answer?

The Day: 15,000 miles

As one of the members of the logistics team, I flew in one week beforehand to help finalize the last day of the walk with the rest of the team. Some of the objectives were to lobby members of Congress about the DREAM ACT (Development, Relief, and a Comprehensive Immigration Reform) and train for civil disobedience.

The day before May 1, we visited the headquarters of UnidosUS (formerly known as LaRaza), an immigration organization based in DC, to learn the history of civil disobedience and how relevant it is in the fight for comprehensive immigration reform. Dr. King once said that "One has a moral responsibility to disobey unjust laws." For Dr. King to succeed in his pursuit of non-violence while bringing awareness to the discrimination and racism that plagued the United States at that time was to use one of the tools Gandhi used to fight oppression in India under the British Empire: civil disobedience.

He understood, as did Gandhi, that lasting change couldn't be achieved through violence. By peacefully subjecting themselves to unjust laws, they demonstrated the oppressors' true nature and highlighted the laws' inherent unreasonableness. In essence, Dr. King's philosophy, as encapsulated in his famous quote, emphasized the importance of following one's conscience over complying with unjust laws.

In many cases in life, we face a reality in which we must choose between obeying our own conscience or certain laws. For me, the walkers and the rest of the team were one of them. How can one consciously accept the fact that approximately 65,000 youths do not get the opportunity to be Americans like many of their peers? They are constantly being called "illegal immigrants." These young people have lived in this country most of their lives, and a majority don't know any country other than the United States. Their primary language is English, they learned and sang the "Star-Spangled Banner" in school, and they want nothing more than to be accepted for who they are… AMERICANS. How can you see them, know their names, call them your friends, minister with them in the church, and yet be able to live your life like nothing is wrong in our society? One of the founders of this nation, Thomas Jefferson, said it best: "When injustice becomes law, resistance becomes duty." We have never been in a better time when resistance is required.

So the walkers had been walking for four months by now, going through communities, talking with many undocumented people, listening to their stories, connecting with their struggles, and even facing KKK members while passing through Georgia. I re-met them on the final walk to reach the White House in DC. We heard the stories, we knew the facts, and we waited and waited for politicians to act. This time we wanted to go a little further, and that's why those of us taking the journey made the decision to engage in civil disobedience by staging a sit-in in front of the White House.

No doubt about it, most of us were scared. The trainers asked us many times if we were to change our minds about moving forward with the action, it was nothing to be ashamed of. Besides the information about civil disobedience, we had to learn some of the laws of the DC police. Once we sat down, they would ask us three times to leave; after that, they would arrest us. We were to wrap our arms with those of the people next to us to create a chain, which would make it more difficult for the police to take us. Earlier that day, we had met with our lawyers to learn how to behave with the police and to have their numbers written on our arms with a permanent marker.

LAKAY

TRAIL OF DREAMS

The Hispanic community often leads the way, when it pertains to immigration reform. In the past, the Haitian community has been noticeably more concentrated on activism than the more recent years. I was proud that we had some Haitian youths take part in the walk on the last day of the demonstration. What is important to recognize is that the immigration issue is not only a Hispanic struggle; it's equally ours as well. It most certainly was mine.

When I was called to speak on the podium on behalf of my community, I took the moment to remind every Haitians, especially the ones who are undocumented by no means should we sit and kick back because we have been granted Temporary Protected Status. This is the speech I delivered that day:

Yesterday, while walking with the group on our way to Washington, DC, I got a phone call from a friend of mine in Miami, who'd run into my mom. told him I was in the Capital, finishing a walk that started in January for immigration reform.

He told me I should be satisfied with the TPS (Temporary Protected Status) and wait for the government to do more.

My question for him yesterday, and for all of us today is: why should I wait? Why should we wait? Why should I be satisfied, and why should you be?

I am not satisfied and won't be satisfied until stories like Oscar's are no more. Still, his pain resonates in my ears. I am not satisfied and won't be satisfied until families across the U.S. can have a good night's sleep without the thought of an ICE agent breaking into their homes.

We started this journey 15,000 miles away, all the way from Miami in front of the Freedom Tower. Like Dr. Martin Luther King Jr. said so profoundly on August 28, 1963, in Washington DC, I am here to remind you of the same thing. Let freedom ring, for all these families living in shadow, let freedom ring for our farmers who are giving their blood in the farms yet still living beyond poverty; let it ring all the way from Miami; let it ring for us, the students who have known this country as our own.

We may be different in our skin colors or languages, but the struggles we face on a daily basis are the same, and we are here to say LOUD AND CLEAR. We are TIRED and WE'VE HAD ENOUGH. UNITED WE STAND!!!

It has been seven years now since I have given that speech in front of the White House. Oh my, how times have truly changed. After one of the most corrupt and inadequate policy driven presidential campaigns, American voters were left with no choice except having to select the lesser of two evils. The general American sentiment was "the devil you know and the devil you don't."doomed if you don't". I How is it that, in theUnited States, is your best choice no solid choice at all?

Donald Trump had anchored his campaign on a premise that shook the very foundation of our community. He vowed to uproot law-abiding, hard-working immigrants from their lives in America and cast them back to their homelands. Under previous administrations, raids occurred under the cover of night – a shroud of darkness where one day you could share laughter with a friend one day, and never see them again.. But now, in a brazen display of power, these raids unfolded in broad daylight. We watched good people, pillars of our community, handcuffed and paraded like felons, their dignity stripped away under the watchful eyes of their children.

Seven years after the walk, I, and so many others, were jolted awake by the harsh reality embedded in the word "Temporary" in Temporary Protected Status (TPS). The rationale for such a designation was to provide sanctuary to immigrants grappling with calamities beyond the control of their governments – be it natural disasters, civil wars, or disease outbreaks. Ironically, the U.S. government, now under a new administration since the era of Donald Trump, had declared that Haiti had sufficiently recovered from the 2010 earthquake. But the American government seemed to be overlooking the cholera outbreak previously cited as justification for the renewal of the TPS program. These soldiers, to this day, remain unaccountable for their actions, while just over a year ago, Hurricane Matthew devastated the South Side of Haiti. Yet, these critical issues garner scant attention, leaving many oblivious to the reality that Haiti is ill-prepared to absorb such a substantial influx of its people returning from the United States.

This decision, made in the halls of power far removed from the lived realities on the ground, seemed indifferent to the lingering scars of Haiti and of those of us who emigrated from there. It disregarded the fragile state of a nation still grappling with the aftermath of disasters, both natural and man-made. The communities in Haiti, striving to rebuild, were scarcely ready to welcome back a wave of deportees, many of whom had spent significant portions of their lives contributing to American society. This policy shift, a stark departure from previous humanitarian considerations, reflected a broader change in the political climate, a change that weighed heavily on mine and others' hearts and minds.

Together with my community, I grappled with uncertainty and fear in the shadow of these decisions. The abrupt shift in policy not only uprooted lives but also unraveled the fabric of families and communities that had been meticulously woven over the years. As advocates and members of these affected communities, we found ourselves questioning the very ideals of justice and compassion that we believed were the cornerstones of American policy. The stories of those involved, the silent pleas of children who feared being torn away from their parents, and the quiet resilience of families facing an uncertain future became the fuel for our continued advocacy. In these stories, we found not just despair, but a steely resolve to fight for a more just and empathetic approach to immigration policy. This resolve transcended political boundaries and spoke to the core of our shared humanity.

A decision like what we have just witnessed reminds us to never lay too low, for at any point it might be too late to react. I remember asking during the Trail of Dreams campaign in 2010, *"Who are you willing to lose? How many people are we willing to lose? WHO are you willing to give up next? Will it be me? Will it be yourself? Is it still OK so long as the person who is taken is someone related to some other individual in a state you've never visited? Is it OK, so long as it isn't any of your friends or your own family?"*

On May 22, 2017, reality didn't just knock; it shattered my door, barreling into my world with an unyielding force. It was the day when former Secretary of Homeland Security John F. Kelly announced the extension of the Temporary Protected Status for Haiti (**only for six months**). This decision profoundly impacted our community. This extension, effective from July 23, 2017, through January 22, 2018, was a pivotal response to Haiti's progress since the devastating earthquake in 2010. Despite the Haitian government's efforts in rebuilding and the significant reduction in internally displaced persons, the limited extension underscored a lingering uncertainty. It stripped me bare, laying open all the fears I shared with my community, leaving us exposed and vulnerable. There was a palpable, suffocating uncertainty about the next six months, reflecting the delicate balance between progress and the ongoing challenges faced by our people. In a mere blink, the fabric of hope and dreams I had woven so meticulously for my family and community was fraying at the edges. For the first time in what seemed like an eternity, the weight of fear loomed more prominent than the resilient spirit of hope that had always buoyed me. Questions swirled in my mind, unceasing and relentless. "Where have I been in these past five years? When did I stray from my path, the path to be a steadfast guardian for my brothers and sisters?"

But just as I teetered on the brink of despair, about to be engulfed by the dark waters of hopelessness, a lifeline of motivation was cast toward me. The sounds of encouragement, initially a distant murmur, crescendoed into a clarion call that rekindled the flame of resolve within me. I found myself slowly regaining my composure, embracing once more the identity I had almost let slip away. The words echoed within me, a mantra of resilience and belief: "We shall overcome, we shall overcome… one day. Oh, deep in my heart, I do believe."

In that moment of rebirth, of renewed momentum, I was reminded of a profound truth. No matter the decisions made that day or six months hence, we, as a community, must resolve that our fight will persevere. This time, our battle cry would transcend the bounds of Temporary Protected Status. We were gearing up for a more significant crusade, one aimed at advocating for comprehensive and humane immigration reform. The sands in the hourglass of the temporary had dwindled; the moment had come for Congress to confront and rectify the fractures in our immigration system.

As I absorbed this newfound light of determination, I realized that our struggle was not just for legal status— it was for recognition of our humanity. We were not mere shadows flitting on the margins of society; we were its very fabric, contributing to its strength and diversity of this great nation. Our fight was not just for ourselves, but for every soul that yearned for dignity, for every voice that sought to be heard, and for every dream that deserved a chance to flourish. It was a clarion call to transform the narrative, to turn the tide from the transient to the enduring, from fear to hope, from division to unity. And in this unyielding spirit, we marched forward, armed with the power of our collective resolve, toward a future where every individual could stand tall, unshackled by uncertainty, embraced by a nation they called home.

Chapter 6

NEVER AGAIN, UN
CHOLERA, A GIFT TO A SURVIVING NATION

CHOLERA, A GIFT TO A SURVIVING NATION

Tuesday, January 12, 2010, is a day that every Haitian remembers like it was yesterday. On an otherwise normal day, around 5:00 p.m., an indescribable sound was heard across Haiti. A massive earthquake with a catastrophic magnitude of 7.0 had stricken the country, with an epicenter near the town of Leogane, which is approximately 25 kilometers west of Port-au-Prince.[2] Within a flash, Leogane, Port-au-Prince, and the neighboring cities were violently shaking. Roofs of houses collapsed instantly, and walls jerked erratically. The falling concrete was crushing and burying people and any other living creature or non-living object. The earth was rumbling down within as if it could swallow everyone. There was nowhere to hide that day. People cried in terror as they tried in vain to save their loved ones.

On that day, thirty-five seconds of unimaginable terror unfolded, a terror so intense it felt like an endless day. As I sat in the U.S., far from my homeland of Haiti, a frightening silence seemed to engulf the entire world. From afar, I learned that thousands of lives, around 230,000, were lost in the blink of an eye. It was a moment when the world seemed to stand still.

Tears and blood were shed by those who barely survived the catastrophe, a scene I could only imagine through the vivid descriptions in the news. People kneeled in prayer or dug through the rubble with their bare hands, desperately searching for their loved ones. Concrete had crushed lives in homes, schools, and hospitals. Over a million were

---

[2] Matt Fisher and Alisha Kramer, "An Epidemic After an Earthquake: The Cholera Outbreak in Haiti, Part 1" (March 7, 2012). Retrieved from https://www.csis.org/blogs/smart-global-health/epidemic-after-earthquake-cholera-outbreak-haiti-part-1

left homeless, their lives forever altered.[3] The concept of luck took on a new, grim meaning. Being lucky meant finding a loved one who hadn't perished. Streets were lined with thousands of bodies awaiting burial in mass graves. The cemeteries and tombs, overwhelmed and unable to accommodate the dead, were a testament to the scale of the tragedy. At funerals, tears had dried up; the reporter from Le Nouvelliste captured the heartbreak, saying, "There were too many of them and not enough tears."[4]

That day, though it happened miles away, changed everything for me, a painful reminder of the fragility of life and the strength of the human spirit

The earthquake left the country in a terrible state. The country's infrastructure was completely destroyed. Roads were ripped apart, electricity supplies were cut, and communication services were destroyed; the country was a shamble. The situation in Haiti called for an immediate intervention in order to help the people cope with the aftershocks of the earthquake. Various institutions, organizations, and agencies came to join hands with the Haitian government to bring relief operations to the crisis. Assistance came from groups such as the United Nations, USAID, the international community, and other humanitarian agencies; the whole country was suffering from lack of food, clothes, and shelter. Hence, there was a need for immediate intervention. Before the earthquake, most people in the country lived in poverty, and with the new challenges facing them, it meant that the level of poverty and other forms of suffering had escalated.

---

3   Katz, J. M. (2016, August 17). *U.N. admits role in cholera epidemic in Haiti*. Retrieved from http://mobile.nytimes.com/2016/08/18/world/americas/united-nations-haiti-cholera.html?0p19G=c

4   Fisher and Kramer, 2012.

Amid ongoing reconstructions by the various groups in Haiti, the country was once again hit by another disaster. It had been barely a year after Haiti experienced the massive earthquake, and they were yet again under the attack of a severe cholera outbreak. The disease had come at such a bad time and so unexpectedly as if to wipe out all the survivors of the earthquake. What could possibly be worse for the people of Haiti? The devastating effects of the earthquake were still fresh in their minds. They had not forgotten the deaths of their loved ones. How could they forget? Yet most of them never got the bodies of their friends and relatives. They were forced to deal with another tragedy: cholera.

The first cholera victim in Haiti was Mr. Palette. The thirty-eight-year-old man woke up normally and went about his daily activities as usual. He went to the Latem River down the hill to take a bath. Children could be seen in the canal washing themselves while others were cleaning their clothes. The water flow which ran up the stream, unknowingly consisted of toxic residue. Nobody would have suspected this danger, since it had been within such close proximity to the UN peacekeeping base. Later that day, he had complained about an aggressive stomach pain. His relatives were unaware of any serious health threat.

A few hours later, he died of cholera. His brother recorded that, "At that time, the word cholera did not exist. By four afternoon on the same day, my brother died. He was the first victim, or so they say." The *New York Times* reported that seventeen months after Mr. Palette died, cholera had already killed 7,050 Haitians and sickened more than 531, 000, which is 5% of the population. The disease continued to spread at lightning speed to every state and neighboring countries, erupting into one of the world's largest cholera epidemics despite the country still dealing with effects of the earthquake.

The spread of the disease was brought about by poor sanitary conditions in the country. Unclean water gives the bacteria the perfect niche to breed and multiply. In Haiti, the environmental conditions were not right, especially after the devastating effects of the earthquake that had been experienced ten months earlier. However, the citizens of Haiti had lived in almost similar conditions for nearly a century without experiencing a cholera outbreak.[5] The sudden appearance of cholera in Haiti raised a number of questions regarding its source. This led to investigations to seek and determine the source of the 2010 cholera outbreak in Haiti. Surveys found that the disease was brought to Haiti by Nepali peacekeepers with the UN.[6] Despite the various research findings suggesting that the peacemakers were responsible for the introduction of the disease in Haiti, the UN continued to deny the claims and refused to take responsibility. They opted to conduct their research, and their results were fabricated in their favor. The UN continued to maintain that the claims that its soldiers were responsible for the introduction of the deadly disease into Haiti were merely unsubstantiated rumors.

The head of the United Nations stabilization mission at that time, Mr. Edmond Mulet, complained, "It is unfair to accuse the UN of bringing cholera to Haiti." Edmond Mulet and other UN officials suggested that the agitators wanted to sow unrest in the country before the upcoming elections, and they were taking advantage of

---

5   Katz (2016).

6   B.R. Archibold and S. Sengupta, "U.N. Struggles to Stem Haiti Cholera Epidemic," *New York Times* (April 19, 2014). Retrieved from http://mobile.nytimes.com/2014/04/20/world/americas/un-struggles-to-stem-haiti-cholera-epidemic.html?referer=http://mobile.nytimes.com/2016/08/18/world/americas/united-nations-haiti-cholera.html?0p19G=c

the issue. However, expert epidemiologic and microbiologic studies found evidence tracing a connection between the cholera trail in Haiti and that of Nepal, but the UN maintained that it was innocent. At the moment, it was hard to know who was telling the truth. It was a blame game between the people and epidemiological experts on one side and the UN on the other. A major eye-opener on the issue came on October 27 when Al Jazeera filmed the UN soldiers with shovels working very hard to contain a sewage spill. A black liquid appeared to be flowing from the latrines at the base into the river.

The UN initially denied responsibility for a cholera outbreak in Haiti. However, after commissioning a new investigation, the UN acknowledged its role, attributing the epidemic to poor sanitation practices by its peacekeepers. The report revealed potential contamination from the base's drainage canal to water sources used by Haitians. Despite the admission, the UN did not fully accept blame for causing the epidemic, and legal immunity was invoked in response to lawsuits. The U.S. government acknowledged the likely involvement of Nepali peacekeepers but emphasized Haiti's poor sanitary conditions. The UN's failure to fully admit responsibility has led to credibility loss, with critics arguing that it contradicts the organization's commitment to human rights. Despite fundraising and efforts to aid Haiti, the country still faces challenges in combating cholera, highlighting ongoing shortcomings in the UN's response.

The misfortune of the 2010 Haitian earthquake, and subsequent cholera epidemic,carried a massive amount of grief. It appears as if whenever there is new optimism to save the people of the island, another unfortunate event transpires, and the optimism fades much faster than it had risen. As it is now, only Haitians can save themselves!

Chapter 7
THE AUDACITY OF FAITH

It was October 10, 2011, a day marked by a clear sky and a sun that held a promise, a stark contrast to the turmoil brewing deep inside me. The clock struck 10:36 a.m. as I stepped out, reluctantly forgoing yet another one of my cherished lab classes. I booked my schedule with back-to-back appointments, a seemingly endless number of offices to visit, and a myriad of people to meet. Each step felt heavier than the last, burdened by the weight of uncertainty and hope.

The first destination on my list was the International Students' Office. I explained my unique predicament, being an in-state student ineligible for FAFSA and not fitting the mold of an international student either – somewhere in between these defined categories. Though not an international student myself, my curiosity and determination had led me there, driven by a quest for answers that seemed to elude me. Alejandro Amaya, a career advisor whose guidance I often sought, had directed me to meet with Ms. Roberta Oreo*[7]. The air in the office was sterile, the walls lined with posters celebrating diversity – a stark contrast to the reception I received.

The visit unraveled in a manner far from what I had hoped. Ms. Oreo's words were laced with thinly veiled condescension, her slick comments cutting through the air. Each time she referred to my status, she used the term "illegal" – a label that stung with every utterance. Yet, with each repetition, I countered firmly, replacing her words with "undocumented." My time as HAYOT president had armed me with enough experience in immigration training and advocacy. I had learned to hold my ground and speak out against such demeaning rhetoric, even when I was seeking assistance.

---

7   * Name was changed for privacy reason

As Ms. Oreo's remarks persisted, my frustration simmered beneath a facade of composure. When she once again carelessly tossed the word "illegal" into the conversation, I could no longer restrain my vexation. "I am not here for that," I retorted, my voice steady yet charged with emotion. "I am more interested in knowing whether you have any scholarships for people in my situation. Let's just stick to that. If you do have scholarships, I would like to know about them, but if you do not, I would like to thank you for your time." Her response was curt and devoid of empathy – they only offered scholarships for international students, and I did not fit that criteria. I met her gaze squarely, I mustered the dignity that her words sought to strip away and said, "Thank you, ma'am."

As I left her office, the door closing behind me felt symbolic, not just of the end of the meeting but of the larger challenges I faced. That interaction was not just about navigating the maze of bureaucracy; it was about maintaining my sense of self in a system that seemed designed to reduce my identity to a label. The audacity of faith was not just a belief in a better future but also in the power of my own voice – a voice that refused to be silenced or categorized, a voice that resonated with the stories and struggles of many like me.

Let love and faithfulness never leave you...write them on the tablet of your heart. (Proverbs 3:3 NIV)

As I left the International Students' office, a sense of resolve settled inside me, tempered by a slight sting of disappointment. I didn't take Ms. Oreo's dismissive attitude personally; rather, I made a mental note to myself. Should I ever cross paths with an international student, I would ensure they knew about this resource, a gesture of guidance I wish had been extended to me.

My next venture led me to the Law Center, nestled in the heart of Building Three on the fourth floor. The corridors were quiet, almost contemplative, as if they, too, were in deep thought about the legal conundrums they housed. I had been here once before, seeking a different service, and had met Ms. Viany, a counselor whose warmth had been a balm to my academic anxieties. She had kindly told me to stop by anytime between the generous hours of 9:00 a.m. to 7:00 p.m. But fate had other plans. Upon my arrival, I was informed that Ms. Viany was out attending to a family emergency. A wave of frustration washed over me. "C'mon, not today…" I thought, with an impatience that gnawed at the edges of my resolve. "Another fruitless visit. Was skipping my reading lab a mistake? Was any of this even worth it?"

But then, as if a switch had been flipped within me, I shook off the cloak of self-pity. This was not the time to wallow in defeat. I recalled a mantra I had long held dear: "Remember, never leave a place without learning something new." As this affirmation resonated in my mind, the receptionist's voice pulled me back to the present. "What can I help you with today?" she inquired with a polite, inquisitive tone.

"It's an academic matter," I responded, cautiously veiling the full extent of my query.

Her next question caught me off guard. "Is it about paralegal studies?" she asked.

"No, but now that you mention it, could you tell me more about that program?" I replied, curiosity piqued by this unexpected turn in our conversation.

"Certainly," she said with a smile that seemed to light up the room. "While you're pursuing your AA in Pre-Law, you only need to take three additional classes to earn your AS in Paralegal Studies."

My spirits lifted at this revelation. "That's fantastic! Do you have any information I could take with me?"

She handed me a pamphlet, its pages a gateway to new possibilities I hadn't considered before. As I left the Law Center, a sense of accomplishment swelled within me. My steps felt lighter, my heart buoyant with newfound knowledge. "You see? You've learned something new. Good job, David!" I congratulated myself, a quiet chuckle escaping my lips. It was moments like these – small victories in the midst of uncertainty – that kept the flame of my aspirations burning bright.

In this journey, each encounter, whether challenging or enlightening, was a stitch in the intricate tapestry of my academic and personal growth. The Law Center, with its network of possibilities, had unexpectedly opened another door, a testament to the unforeseen paths that often emerge when we least expect them. As I navigated the corridors of the university, each step was a reminder that every day held the potential for new lessons, new opportunities, and new horizons to explore.

Delight yourself in the Lord and He will give you the desires of your heart. (Psalm 37:4 ESV)

After that visit, I was supposed to go to Wells Fargo to do a withdrawal for my dad. However, because these two visits did not turn out the way I expected, I decided to go to the financial aid office. The office was a bustling hub of aspirations and anxiety,, each student walking through the door carrying their own unique story. I approached the front desk where Ms. Margarita, a sweet Haitian lady, greeted me with a warm, albeit puzzled, smile. Her presence, a comforting reminder of home, eased some of my apprehension. "I would like to know if there is any scholarship that I would be eligible for," I inquired, my voice steady yet laden with the weight of my situation.

Ms. Margarita's expression transformed into one of confusion, her eyes narrowing, her lips parting slightly as if grappling to grasp the gravity of my request. "What do you mean? Can you elaborate a little?" she asked, leaning forward with a genuine desire to understand.

Her response, though tinged with regret, carried a glimmer of hope. "Unfortunately, there is not much I can do. However," she leaned back, her posture reflecting a mix of contemplation and determination, "I know the college has funds for students like you, but you need to register early."

Her advice took a surprising turn. She observed me closely, noting, "You look reliable and trustworthy. Your attire sets you apart from most who come here." A faint smile crossed my lips, but I remained focused on her words.

"You should consider volunteering at strategic offices," she continued, her gaze intense, her words imbued with wisdom. "Visit the book fair at the International Office, the president's office, Miami Dade College Lawyers, and the law center. These places are where you can make key contacts while working on your future."

Her advice was a guiding light, illuminating a path I hadn't considered. She emphasized the importance of being proactive and of making a strong impression. "Go with questions, give a firm handshake, and let them see the person behind the handshake."

As our conversation drew to a close, my once-blank sheet of paper was now a treasure trove of names, office addresses, and invaluable advice. I stepped out of the office, not just overjoyed but empowered, ready to embark on this new adventure. Ms. Margarita had not just given me directions; she had bestowed upon me a strategy, a way to navigate the intricate puzzle of academia and life beyond, bridging the gap between my present uncertainties and future aspirations.

As I walked down the hall, her words reverberated in my mind, a mantra for the days ahead. Each office she mentioned was not just a location but a gateway to possibilities. With a renewed sense of purpose and determination, I set forth, ready to turn these possibilities into realities.

Meeting the Officials

On October 12, 2011, two days following my fascinating conversation with Margarita, I embarked on a quest to explore the four offices she had recommended. The day, imbued with a sense of purpose, coincided with a job fair on campus – an event that my then-college survival skills professor, Ms. Sindy Eugene, had urged us to attend. She had tasked us with writing a reflective piece on our experience, advising us to dress professionally and arm ourselves with at least three resumes, ready to be handed to prospective employers.

My academic morning concluded with a reading class led by Professor Daphne Gilles. Upon its completion, I dove into the lively atmosphere of the job fair. I navigated through the multitude of company booths, engaging with representatives and collecting business cards as tangible evidence of my visit. Each interaction was a brushstroke in the portrait of my future aspirations. Though I managed to draft a reflective paper for Ms. Eugene, time was pressing, and I reluctantly tore myself away to fulfill my commitment to visiting the recommended offices.

The Law Center was my first stop. Once again, I sought Ms. Viany, only to learn she was out for lunch. A receptionist, a beautiful young black lady with an air of quiet efficiency, suggested I return at 1:00 p.m. Although unsure of my ability to revisit that day, I acknowledged her advice. As I made my way to the elevator, my thoughts had already transitioned to the next destination: the book fair in the international office.

The office was in Building Four, a space that seemed to breathe with the pulse of global cultures. I found myself speaking with a young Spanish woman whose long, curly brown hair cascaded down her slender back. Her initial hesitation at my request gave way to curiosity, and she excused herself to check the director's availability. Upon returning, she inquired about the nature of my visit. With renewed confidence, I extended my hand, introducing myself and expressing my interest in volunteering for the fair. She directed me to Stephanie Farokhnia, the Operational Assistant of the Miami Book Fair International at that time. Stephanie's response was pragmatic – assigning me to assist with the backstage preparations, a task I accepted with gratitude and a firm handshake.

Energized, I continued to Building One, where the office of Miami Dade College Lawyers resided. Stepping into the shared space with the board, I felt a surge of confidence. Ms. Nannette Orange, the paralegal, listened attentively as I explained my intent. However, her response carried a tinge of disappointment. "Unfortunately, two things are working against you," she began. My heart sank, and a sudden wave of anxiety washed over me. She detailed the lack of available space for volunteers and the preference for interns. Despite this, she offered a glimmer of hope, promising to speak with a lawyer on my behalf.

As I left the office, my feelings were a complex wave of hope, uncertainty, and determination. Each interaction, each conversation, was a stepping stone, a chapter in my story of persistence and resilience. The walk through the campus, from one office to another, was more than a physical traverse; it was an odyssey of self-discovery, of understanding the intricacies of navigating a world that often felt tangled. As I prepared to return on Monday, I carried with me not just the names and advice scribbled on my sheet but also the lessons gleaned from each encounter – lessons of perseverance, adaptability, and the unyielding spirit of ambition.

> *Trust in the Lord with all your heart... In all your ways acknowledge him, and he will make straight your paths.*
> *(Proverbs 3:5–6 ESV)*

After that meeting, I was like a zombie in *The Walking Dead*. The only thing I could do was to keep moving forward even though I did not have a concrete goal in mind. Before I ended the day, I went to my last office. Like a phoenix, I had to be reborn from the ashes of my own despair and discouragement. In 2 Corinthians 4:8–9 (NIV), Apostle Paul said: "We are pressed on every side, but not crushed; perplexed, but not in despair; persecuted, but not abandoned; struck down, but not destroyed." I could not find better words of encouragement at the moment. Every way I turned, I was pressed hard by all those "no's," yet I was not crushed.

I took the elevator to the fourth floor in the same building to see if I could meet with Mr. Padron, president of the college. I introduced myself and asked if I could speak with the president. The receptionist refused because he was in a meeting. While talking with her, I saw Mr. Padron passing by. I ran after him, but he had another meeting to attend in fifteen minutes. He was rushing to make it, but he asked me to leave a note at the desk and said that he would contact me when he returned. I went back inside, and left my name, my student ID number, my phone number, and the reason for my visit.

I said to myself, "How can a day that I started being well prepared and full of enthusiasm end this way?" While leaving the president's office, I asked myself, "Why not stop by the office of Professor Frank Pradel?" He used to be one of my EAP (English for Academic Purposes) professors. As always, he was happy to see me. He asked me how I was doing with school, and because he knew my immigration status, he asked me if I had been able to find some help paying for classes. I said no. He said, "Let me call the vice president's office on campus... Mr. Montoya."

He called him and explained my situation. Mr. Montoya said, "There might be certain things available to him. Ask him to go see Mr. Rulx Jean-Bart, the director of admissions and registration."

I went there and talked to Mr. Jean-Bart. He informed me that the real people to talk to were Mr. Bien-Aime Lehman and Ms. Lyne Darius, both counselors at the financial aid office. I went to them, but unfortunately, they were also of no help. However, they did tell me to talk to the director of financial aid, Mr. Daphnis. Ms. Lyne said, "It seems you have high-level contacts; ask Mr. Montoya to call Mr. Daphnis so you don't have to wait."

I went back to Professor Pradel and asked him to call Mr. Montoya again. Professor Pradel called Mr. Monaud Daphnis directly and told him that he had spoken to Mr. Montoya about my issue and asked if he could help me. Mr. Daphnis told Professor Pradel to tell me to come see him.

After running around all day, I was slightly relieved but still a little skeptical. While heading to his office, I checked my watch and saw that it was 12:55 p.m. My Christian club meeting was at 1:00 p.m. I prayed to God, "I have to be in both places right now, but I'm choosing to go to the club meeting. Make Mr. Daphnis wait for me." When I got to the room, I found three other students waiting. We began with prayer and then read and prayed over Isaiah 54:1–2; 1 Chronicles 4:10, and 2 Corinthians. 8:9—which happen to focus on God's promise to give prosperity.

One verse in Hebrews proclaims that God puts His words above Himself. Therefore, it was only strategic to pray with words. I went to see Mr. Daphnis after the Bible study, and God answered the prayer I'd made on my way to the Bible study. I went to his office, introduced myself, and gave him a firm handshake. He told me that he had been waiting for me for more than an hour. I apologized for the delay and explained my situation. "I am not an expert in immigration," he replied. "However, bring all the immigration papers that you have," he replied. "I will have our immigration expert look at them and see what comes back. Why don't we meet next Friday at 9:30 a.m.?"

As I was walking back to Mr. Pradel's office, a quote I'd read a while ago came to my mind. "Many of the greatest achievements of the world were accomplished by tired and discouraged people who kept working." This quote encapsulated my journey in looking for financial aid for college. My question for you is: What is stopping you today? What did people tell you that you cannot do or achieve? Who DARES to tell you not to dream or to stop looking? I am telling you right now that you can go further than where your friends stopped. You can reach higher than where your family stopped. Wherever there is a NO, there is a YES. You just have to keep looking and keep talking to the right people with the right title and at the right time.

For our heart shall rejoice in Him because we have trusted in His holy name. (Psalms 33:21 KJB)

Faith

After I'd spent a year praying and going from one office to another, God opened a door I did not know existed. It all began a month before, October 2, 2011, when I heard God whisper in my heart, "This semester you are going to school, and you will not have to pay a dime out of your own pocket." I was reluctant to read that verse: "Delight yourself in the Lord and He will give you the desires of your heart" (Psalm 3:4 NASB). But I had to believe.

Three weeks after I met with Mr. Daphnis to give him my immigration papers, I stopped by his office for an update. When I got there, it was about 1:45 p.m. The receptionist said he was on the phone but that I could wait for him if I wanted to. "Sure, not a problem," I replied. One hour passed, and I was still waiting. He finally arrived around 2:50 p.m. He was glad to see me and asked me to follow him to his office. I sat down, and he asked me for my student ID. A few seconds passed, and I saw his eyes grow wider. His eyebrows dropped a little to focus on something. Then he told me, "I might have good news." His eyes still looking at the screen, he said again, "I might have good news." He said it for a third time while he turned his eyes away from the screen: "I might have good news." He turned the computer screen towards me while pointing at something and scrolling down to show me what he was talking about. He then told me, "When you see that section checked, the student can get financial aid. You got it, David, you got it."

I asked him, "What should I do next?"

"Jump up and down," he replied.

Through this journey to find financial aid for my classes, I met four different kinds of people:

- The one who knows but hides the information from you
- The one who does not know but is super rude and does not care about you
- The one who does not know but will try their best to help you
- The one who knows and will go the extra mile to help you

> *I will place on his shoulder the key of the house of David; what he opens no one can shut, and what he shuts no one can open. (Isaiah 22:22 NIV)*

Having faith is akin to nurturing a fragile flame amid a storm. It is one thing to hold on to faith when the path is clear, but quite another to cling to it when engulfed in shadows, where the more likely outcomes mock your aspirations. In this arena where logic grapples with faith, a battleground emerges from the threads of probability and possibility. Doubts, those insidious visitors, often knock on the door, cloaked as allies of comfort and complacency. Yet, in these moments of uncertainty, faith demands we step outside our comfort zones. This kind of audacious faith has sculpted me, molding my perspective and resilience in ways nothing else ever could. It propelled me to view the world through a different lens – one where rejection was merely a detour, not a dead end, and where my belief in Jehovah Jireh, the Provider, remained unshakable.

I embraced the belief that the best work is done today, taking small but significant bites out of my ambitions each day. My eyes remained fixated on the finish line, not the hurdles strewn along the path. There were times when the temptation to abandon my journey was as vital as air to my lungs, yet the true exhilaration, the purest breath of fresh air, came from moments of triumph, from inhaling the glory of persistence.

Repeated rejections have been part of my journey, each 'no' a stepping stone rather than a setback. Through the audacity of keeping the faith, I found courage in the battle against my greatest opponent – myself. Despite others pointing out my accent or questioning my paperwork, my heart remained steadfast, my purpose resolute, my goal unwavering. Greater is the spirit of God within me, a beacon guiding me through the tumultuous seas of doubt and uncertainty.

Now, I implore you, reader – never settle, never back down. Keep pushing toward that dream, that diploma, that career. Embrace the scripture, "They shall come out against you one way and flee before you seven ways" (Deuteronomy 28:7 ESV). Your potential is boundless because it springs from a limitless source. Press on, just as I have, for I am convinced that neither life, nor angels, nor principalities, nor present nor future, nor any height or depth, nor any creature in all creation, can sever you from the destiny that awaits you. Today, I stand as a testament to the power of daring to believe, a living embodiment of hope found in the Audacity Of Faith.

Chapter 8
BRIDGING DREAMS AND REALITY: MY YEAR UP EXPERIENCE

I was assisting in the closing ceremony of Connect to Complete, a program where sophomore students mentor incoming freshmen, with my two mentees from the program, when Janelle Viruet and Vanessa Grover pitched the Year Up program. At the time, Janelle was the internship coordinator and Vanessa was the admission coordinator. Upon entering the room, they passed out these glossy flyers to every table, and the one phrase that jumped out at me was, "Earn while you learn." For me, as a scholar, there was nothing more divine than those four words basically telling me that I could get paid for going to school. A few minutes later, they got on stage to explain in further detail about Year Up, and how the program worked.

When the event was over, I excitedly rushed home and gleefully shared with Elpidia, my wife and then-girlfriend, what I had heard from these two-people representing a new fascinating organization coming to Wolfson. I convinced her that it was a great program and urged her to send an email to Vanessa, one of the people in charge, to express her interest. She did. A day or two passed as we anxiously waited, and she finally got a call from Vanessa who invited her to the open house. Elpidia begged me to go with her, but before I agreed, I made it clear to her; even though the prospect was extremely compelling, I was already committed to my other activities and did not feel I could give them up. My plate was full with me being a full-time student with a part-time job while leading a Christian and academic club on campus, not to mention my duties to my church. I reiterated that there was no way that I could do this program on top of all my other responsibilities.

She conceded and said, "Fine, you don't have to apply. But you do have to come with me."

I reluctantly accepted. The open house was in the advising office on campus in a small conference room with a thirty-inch television and a long rectangular table in the middle of the room. We all apprehensively sat down to get a better understanding of Year Up, the whole "earn while you learn" thing.

Some of the people from the program who were in that room with me were Janelle Viruet, Vanessa Grover, Lisette Nieves, and Carlos Vazquez,who had just flown up from San Francisco the night before).. There were also other students who were interested in learning a bit more about the program, besides myself and Elpidia: a student named Eric, one named Anthony who had just moved from Orlando, and one named Niva.

Vanessa and Janelle welcomed us to the meeting and introduced Lisette, who at the time was Director of Strategy and Programs. She explained what Year Up was, and expanded deeper into the benefit of what a program like this could provide for the applicants. At the time, I loftily thought this did not pertain to me, for I was definitely not applying. To further convince the actual applicants (not me of course), they played testimonial videos about three students who professed how Year Up had helped them change their lives for the better.

Once the presentation was done, those who were interested could apply for the programThey passed the paper to Elpidia, she wrote her name and, being her naturally steadfast self, she wrote my name under hers. From my seat, right across the table from her, I gave her an incredulous look. She responded with a shrug and whispered to me, "You are here. Why don't you just sign up?" They passed out some other forms in order to determine whether the attendees were working, to gain information about direct deposit, etc. This time, when one of the staff members gave me that paper, I nervously looked at Elpidia for a quick second while processing in my mind the fact that I was really signing up for this program. While I thought it was a great program, at the time I was already incredibly busy and working at Nike at the Dolphin Mall. I needed that job, and it didn't seem plausible to add yet another program to my plate. But after she gave me a quick nod of encouragement, I firmly held the yellow and blue Year Up pen and boldly filled out the forms.

When everything was done, they asked Elpidia and I if we'd have time to interview that very same day. Our conflicting schedules did not allow it, so we scheduled our interviews for later in the week. While leaving, I tried to talk myself out of it, thinking to myself, "I don't see myself with a computer major or a business. This program does not fit me. I can see myself doing only two things: politics or law. That's what I've always wanted to do and what I'm going to do." Yet something inside me nudged me to power through the application process because I did truly believe that it was a good program. After all, from a strictly financial standpoint, getting the stipend would not hurt my pocket. Before I finally convinced myself to make the commitment, I made sure that I understood the sacrifices and hard work this year-long commitment would entail. I was going to have to adjust everything around this program if I were to be accepted into it. For me, it was a binding decision, and quitting was not an option.

We returned later that week for our interviews. We dressed professionally to meet with the staff in the Miami Dade College-Wolfson Campus building. Elpidia went to the second floor to be interviewed by Carlos, while I stayed on the first floor to be interviewed by Janelle and Lisette, who I'd met at the previous meeting.

Elpidia and I both thought we interviewed well. The next and final phase of the application process was to write an essay sharing our story, and why we believed we should be accepted to the program. We did so, and sent the essays to Vanessa.

A few days later, Elpidia received the news that she was not accepted—she had already accumulated too many college credits and was already close to graduating. Ironically enough, I was accepted, and I remember laughing to myself thinking how funny it was that I had not even wanted to apply for this program in the first place.

In retrospect, from the moment I was accepted into the program, I decided that I was going to make it my utmost priority and give it nothing but my very best. That included being a role model, punctual, and a true optimist. I wanted to do it primarily for myself, though my family, mostly my mom and dad, were always my driving force.

Now, when I serve as a guest speaker or simply advise current students or interns, one of the questions they always ask me is, "How was it being the first Year Up class?" I, in turn, always give them the same answer: "It was hectic and super cool at the same time." As part of Class One, we had many—and I mean *many*—challenges and hurdles to overcome. The staff had just moved to Miami, the program's first year in a new town, and the Professional Training Course model was still in its developing stage. For the program to be successful, it depended on the students as much as it did on the staff. At first, the energy was there; everyone was giving 110 percent, even when most of us were struggling to wake up at the crack of dawn to arrive to class on time because every second counts when one is running against the clock. Most of us were still getting used to wearing professional clothes on campus in contrast to our standard casual shirts and jeans attire, which was a requirement of the Year Up program. Yet, we persevered.

There was something about Year Up that any other program, not even the MDC Honors program, simply did not provide. For me, Year Up handed us the tools needed to bring value to employers. It's the small details that people do not usually spend time on that make the big difference, such as being on time all the time (surveys show that most people are not fired for incompetence but for tardiness), being present mentally and physically once in the room, networking, code switching, and other helpful tools.

Even with a program as great as Year Up, the challenges we faced as the first class were second to none. There was no precedent to follow in Year Up Miami; thus, we were paving the very first stones that would set the standard for this new iteration of the program. Mistakes were made and corrected as we powered forward. However, some of my colleagues did not do anything to help, so eventually, discouragement and impatience kicked in. We wanted everything right then and there, which often frustrated the staff because, in their eyes, they were doing everything they could to help. Vanessa would constantly be on the phone trying to fix the schedule of one of my classmates while simultaneously getting hammered for another unintended issue. Carlos was still trying to find a better way of giving us feedback while being accused of playing favorites. Janelle still faced pressure securing enough internship spots for all of us in a city where the program was still trying to gain footing with employers.

Now, Year Up South Florida (Previously named Year Up Miami) is working well on all cylinders; almost everything is working to perfection. They have even become stricter about the requirements to get into the program. More students are signing up, employers are asking for more interns every cycle, and the staff is growing every year. In my time, any major could apply; you just had to be eighteen to twenty-four years old with fewer than thirty college credits. Now, you must have already declared a major in IT or business.

Looking back, our inaugural class was able to create a platform for the future of Year Up South Florida. The program has proven its value outside of Florida, and has hit major areas like Philadelphia, San Francisco Bay Area, Jacksonville, Arizona, and Dallas, and continues to grow and help various students across the country.

In my opinion, the success of the program came down to how much they truly cared about us. I remember going through some financial hurdles while in the program, and was unable to pay my tuition to stay in the program. As a last hope, I reached out to the Year Up staff, specifically Vanessa. She referred me to Lisette and advised me to write her a letter about what I was going through. Following is the text of that letter:

4/16/13

My name is David Frederick, and I am a student at Miami Dade College, Wolfson Campus. I am a double major in Pre-Law (AA) and Paralegal Studies (AS) due to graduate in summer 2013. I'm the fifth child in a family of seven. Like most of the boys at that time, I found enjoyment and pleasure not in playing Nintendo, PlayStation, or Xbox, but manufacturing small cars with cans and running around the neighborhood with a wheel and a hanger in my hand. After school, I would go home to study and do my homework despite not having anything to eat or electricity for light to study. Coming to the United States was probably one of the hardest choices I have ever made, yet the most courageous choice by far. Being in Miami Dade College is already considered a miracle, and paying for it every semester is a grace beyond measure.

At first, my mom and my sister were the only ones working to pay the rent and all of the bills in the house. Fortunately, my brothers and I got a job. We have been trying to help out as much as possible. Due to the instability of my mom's and my sister's jobs, we always find ourselves coming up short at the end of the month to pay the bills. As a result, we moved from house to house-- a year here, two years there, etc. At one point, I asked myself, "Why should I have to choose between a roof on top of my head and my future?" Despite the inherent frustration in this question, I found a way to motivate myself. I made sure that I worked twice as hard as anybody else wherever I went, talked with my professors to see what kind of scholarship could benefit me, or who they might know that can help me. In every step that I made, I strove for excellence. Nevertheless, the realities of life were still with me.

As a student who pays for most of his classes out of his pocket, it has been difficult to fully focus in class since the possibility of having classes dropped continues to worry me. It has been disheartening to go through this since this possibility is not due to lack of interest or motivation. Despite the challenges, I have remained optimistic and positive. This scholarship will not only keep me in school, it will help me to finally find an answer to a question that has been pursuing me for a long time: "The roof or the future?"

In my few weeks at Year Up, I have already learned that they are not interested in giving a handout to people, rather holding you accountable by providing high support and in return having high expectations of the individual. I am also driven by the motto of Miami Dade College, which is "Opportunity Is Everything," in a world where the race is won not by the smartest and the fastest all the time, but by the number of opportunities one takes advantage of. This scholarship will help me finish my degree in Miami Dade College and will give me a boost to continue working hard while I aim to attend FIU, Florida International University, to get my bachelor's degree in International Relations. After FIU I intend to apply for law school at Georgetown University and specialize in international law. I have chosen Georgetown University because of their prestigious law school program and also to challenge myself to be more than just an ordinary lawyer.

As a Haitian immigrant, I know the challenges that my fellow brothers and sisters are facing on a daily basis. Earning an international law degree will provide me with the necessary knowledge to assist them in their daily difficulties. I also intend to go back to Haiti in order to give my people the same opportunity I have been given here in the United States and help the government develop a more robust education system to ensure the safeguard of the generation that will come after us.

Soon after I sent the letter, Ms. Nieves agreed to help me on behalf of Year Up. I mentioned this story and published the letter because I want you to know that the reason this organization is successful and has now become a major actor in closing the opportunity divide is very simple: they care. We, the students, are truly their priority. For Year Up, "student first" is more than a tagline; it's a culture. It's at the center of their moral compass. It's who they are.

A Day in the Life of a first year Year Up student:

One of my biggest mind challenges in the program was having to go to work after Pro-Skills, the oh-so-riveting four-hour tech class. I particularly remember one day that made it seem virtually impossible to keep on with the program. It began like any typical Miami day; breezy December day, just what one could expect.

I took the Transit Miami public bus right in front of MDC-Wolfson and headed south to the Dolphin Mall in Doral where I was working as a sales associate at the Nike store at that time. The position required me to be standing and running on my feet during the entirety of my six-hour shift with only a thirty-minute break. Mind you, this is after having to wake up at 5:00 a.m. to catch the bus in North Miami to make it downtown to the MDC-Wolfson campus for my 8:00 a.m. Computer Essentials class and then enduring the tedious Pro-Skills class. I only had a 30-minute break in a fifteen-hour day that entailed covering vast distances in the City of Miami. Moreover, once my shift was done, I trudged to the bus station to catch my bus, but as misfortune would have it, it was running late. By the time the bus arrived, I was unable to get the transfer bus to get me home to North Miami. Unfortunately, the expected December chill kicked in, and I only had my Nike black and white striped polo shirt to keep me warm. Every store in the area was closed, so I could not even buy a light jacket to protect me from the low sixty-degree chill. I was forced to stand by a tree to take refuge from the winds that were gusting at thirty miles per hour.

My frustration and fatigue were at an all-time high that day, and the only thing on my mind was to quit Year Up and *Nike*, find something closer to home, and work elsewhere. I had had enough! But I'm not a quitter, and my distaste for not finishing something I had started trumped my frustrations. I am not one to give my word and commitment and then walk away when the road gets a little too tough to handle. Whatever I start, I make sure to finish. That is why it gets under my skin when people give up before they even get started. That is what I see in the majority of people today. They get involved in things, give their commitment to a project, get accepted in a certain place, and then, when the road gets tough, they bounce! If the process is not what they anticipated, they just quit! In my eyes, people quit when they are not proud of their work and are thinking only about themselves. Today's society does not help, for we live in an individualistic world in which everything is ME, Myself, and I. I could not afford that mentality, for it was more than just "me" on this road. It was about my valiant mother, who tirelessly spent years struggling to give me a better education, put food in my belly, and ensure we always have a roof over our heads. My determined father, who sacrificed himself to live in a politically and economically unstable country to provide for his children. My ambitious then-girlfriend who has not lost her drive as my graceful wife, who supports and motivates me daily. That is why I did not quit that cold December night as I was forced to wait an extra hour for the next bus, thus delaying my trip home by two hours. This particularly strenuous twenty-two hours reminded me that the journey is not solely about me, and sometimes the process is not going to be the way I'd envisioned it—and that's fine. I chose to persevere and stay focused.

My Internship at AT&T:

At this time, the Year Up program looked like this: six months of learning and development skills, where we learned computer science and business. The second half of the year was when the staff matched us with a corporate partner. As the days passed, the internships were due to be announced. Everyone was ecstatic and was wondering who was going where.

Unfortunately, I went to work on the day the staff announced the internship placements. When I came to class the next day, I heard that I had been placed at AT&T, and, frankly, I did not know what to expect.

It might sound strange, but at the time I barely knew anything about AT&T and what they did. In hindsight, not knowing anything about a company that has been in existence for more than a century and has been part of every breakthrough in telecommunications seems crazy. (I only knew about Metro PCS—that's what I could afford.) So when I said that I really didn't know what to expect, I really did not.

On my first day, I walked into AT&T filled with excitement and anxiety, I was greeted in the lobby by Ms. Hope Todoroff, a sweet middle-aged woman who was the secretary for Mr. Robert Suarez, the Director of the Southeast Region. After a short and friendly introduction, we went upstairs where she gave me a brief tour of the office. A few minutes later, Mr. Suarez walked in, he called me to his office, gave me a firm handshake, and we started talking about our backgrounds and Year Up.

Once I walked back to my cubicle, I saw a book on my desk entitled *Obstacles Welcome*, by Ralph De La Vega, the former president and CEO of AT&T Mobility. "It's for you, David. It's a very good book, and I hope you read it," Ms. Hope said.

"Sure, I will. Thanks a lot," I replied.

I was hooked on the book from the moment I opened it. I simply could not put it down. As I read about the way De La Vegae came into this country and what he had to overcome,, I could not help but think about myself and other people who came to this country to have a better life to ensure that their families succeed and prosper.. I thought about the possibilities that a country like the United States offers. As good as the book was to read, I had to do what I was here to do, which was work.

I pulled my chair forward to be a bit closer to the computer and typed my username and password given to me earlier by Ms. Hope. From day one, I knew the internship was not a playground where I would joke here and there and wait for the time to pass by.

Year Up had given me the key and showed me a door that I did not know existed; it was an opportunity like no other. The internship was six months for me to prove myself, to strengthen my skills, and to mold myself into a young professional. I could have messed up on day one, day twenty-five, or day fifty-five, but I had six months to add value to the workplace, meaning I had six months to interview for the job.

My responsibilities during the internship consisted of the following:

- Sending a text page to the technicians on the field reminding them about the service level agreement (SLA)
- Conducting quality tool inventory weekly for the ten worst technicians under Mr. Robert Suarez's organization
- Assisting my supervisor with audits, such as number of vehicles available for surplus and capital tool inventory
- Weekly field safety visits with the technicians

Every day when I went to work I sent the SLAs, checked the reports to find the ten worst technicians to see where they needed to improve and focus, and called my supervisor to see if there were any vehicles that needed to be surplus. Some days when Mr. Suarez had a meeting, he would ask me to attend the meeting so that I would have a better view of what the business was and how the work I was doing impacted the team in a positive way. Before or after the meeting, he would share some perspective on why he had or not done something. He included me in almost every conversation and made me feel that I was not just an intern but also a vital part of the team. When he took the staff to lunch or had meetings with them, Mr. Suarez or Ms. Hope would always encourage me to come. They saw in me a son, and I saw in them strong mentors who were trying to pull out the potential they saw in me. At times, they would even ask me to lead and share my story when students visited the building as part of the "Aspire" program.

I also received that respect when I was on the weekly field safety visits with the technicians. They knew that I was there on behalf of the director; therefore, they treated me with respect.

Through it all, I always made sure I was punctual and did my work to the best of my ability. I knew to never get too comfortable in a way that would interfere with my work or my attendance. It was something Year Up staff had always reminded us about time and again: know your boundaries and make it clear. Even when they treated me like one of their own, I treated them like my superiors. I was wise enough to walk away when I was no longer part of the conversation. Little did I know, I was leaving a strong impression of my brand for the duration of the internship.

Every time my schedule freed up, I was glued to the book. I yearned to know how Ralph De La Vega had overcome his trials and tribulations. In the end, I came to realize that his strategy was that he saw every challenge as the next opportunity in disguise. He never limited himself to only seeing the problem; instead, he saw the project behind it. He found a way to relearn things.

The world is forever changing. I can either change with it and spot the next opportunity or be an observer and watch other people become successful. I choose the former. Looking back, this is one of the greatest gifts I could have ever received from the staff.

Walk for Opportunity:

The walk for opportunity was a historic step in Year Up's journey for social change and economic prosperity and the belief that, to galvanize the U.S. economy, we must connect America's skilled urban young adults with the businesses that need their talent. That day my class met with some of the students from Class Two, the staff, and some local partners to start walking from the Year Up offices in the MDC-Wolfson Building Five to Building Two where the stage was located, and where other families, friends, and supporters of the program were waiting for us. As it is the custom of any Year Up event to include the student, I was selected by the staff to speak on both the national theme, "Recognizing Talent," and our local site theme, "Diversity." What follows is the speech I gave on recognizing talent and on diversity:

> *Right now, six million young adults with no more than a high school diploma are out of work, out of school, and without access to the economic mainstream. They have talent. On the other side, fourteen million jobs requiring post-secondary education will go unfilled in the next decade. How? According to Pew Research Center, "Roughly ten thousand baby boomers are reaching retirement age every day; more will cross that threshold every day for the next nineteen years." This is a crisis where in one part of the tower millions of young adults are looking for opportunity, and on the other side millions of jobs are looking for talent. What we are asking as young people is very simple: give us the opportunity to bring value to your workplace. We are not asking for favors, nor do we ask for a handout. We are asking for a hand up, knowing we have to work hard from start to finish. We knew it already, and we are committed to making it happen. We've proved it through Year Up where 84% of Year Up students are employed or in college full-time within four months of their Year Up graduation. Moreover, Kirten Wolberg, the CIO of Salesforce*

says, "We brought five interns into Salesforce, and every single one of them immediately started to add value in the department and the areas that they were in." They need us as much as we need them.

We are not only here to talk about opportunity; we are also here to celebrate our rich diversity. Haiti's slogan says, "L'union fait la force," which means "Unity Is Strength." Our differences should never divide us, but unite us. It should make us stronger, better as a community. Let's celebrate and admire this diversity throughout our communities, our campuses, and churches. Let's embrace it as strength not a weakness, as a weapon to overcome challenges not one to destroy our communities. In Year Up we don't just talk about it, we're doing it. We are all diverse individuals; celebrating it and recognizing it can and will surely be one of the keys to transform a workplace. Statistics illustrate how skewed the population is, for 60% black; 21% Hispanic; 5% White; 4% Asian, and 10% all classify themselves as other. Furthermore, all of us in Year Up Class One Miami speak more than one language. We all will bring diversity in color, language, culture, and mindset. For the economic race doesn't happen on the national level anymore; it's international, it's global. To win, you need diversity and talents.

The Hiring Process at AT&T:

After a few weeks of interning at AT&T under Mr. Suarez, I had been told that he wanted me to be an AT&T employee. He advised me to take the technician exam, which I did; but unfortunately, I did not pass the test. Like any great **MULTIPLIER** boss, he reminded me that there were other departments that I could apply to if I still wanted to be part of the AT&T family. One of the departments was mobility. After four months of interning with Mr. Suarez, I took and passed the online assessment for AT&T Mobility. Now I was waiting to get a call from the hiring manager for the area to do a face-to-face interview. After three days, he finally called me, and I met with him. From the feedback he gave me following the interview, everything had gone well and I should be expecting a call from the store manager to have a final meeting.

Two days after my interview with the hiring manager, I got my first call from a store in Fort Lauderdale. Even though I lived in North Miami, my desperation to get the job superseded the distance to travel to the job five days a week. I left the interview knowing that I had gotten the job because I had had a great conversation and a convincing argument for why I should be the one hired. A day passed, nothing; another day, nada. A whole week and not a word. I called the area manager who informed me they had chosen to go with someone else. I thanked him for the opportunity, but I knew I could not stop there. I was too close to give up now. I spoke to Mr. Suarez and Ms. Hope about it, and they both encouraged me to keep trying.

A week later, which was one month before I finished my internship, I got another call from the hiring manager to meet with the manager at the AT&T Biscayne store. I went to that interview knowing it was a wrap. The store was in North Miami, which is full of Haitians. I speak Creole, French, and English. I polished my resume, printed it on nice paper, and put it in a folder. After the interview, in order to stand out from everyone who may have come before and would be coming after me, I gave the manager a thank you note. That was my icing on the cake. I left with a big smile on my face. The next day, I told Ms. Hope how I did and how confident I was. She was very excited because they all wanted me to stay with the company.

After a week and a half of waiting, I called, and yet again the store manager had chosen to go with a different candidate. Despite my disappointment, I thanked her again for the opportunity and hung up. I went to Mr. Suarez to let him know where I was because he had told me to keep him posted on everything. He shared his disappointment and told me, "Throughout my career at AT&T, if there is one person I am sure of, it's YOU." Looking me straight in the eyes, he continued to say, "I have no doubt that you will be an asset for AT&T; you are a clear example of someone AT&T should not let go of."

"Thank you very much. I really appreciate these words," I replied.

A few minutes passed; he came to my cubicle and told me to follow him. We went to his counterpart, Mr. Frank Castaneda, the former director of mobility for the Southeast. We sat in the office, and Mr. Suarez asked me to introduce myself and talk about the Year Up program. I was so caught up in the moment that it was hard for me to find the right words. Mr. Suarez wasted no time in taking over and explaining what Year Up does, what I had been doing for him in his department, and how strongly he believed that I would be an asset to the company. He also mentioned that I spoke Creole, French, and English, and that I could understand some Spanish.

I was so shocked, I could not believe what he just did. Usually, when someone appreciates what you have done for them, they tend to send a letter of recommendation or make a call. This time, Mr. Suarez went above and beyond all measures to make sure I was hired. He put his name and all his years of experience on the line for me. In that meeting, the only thing I had said was, "My name is David Frederick." Everything else came from Mr. Suarez's mouth.

I left the room in awe over how someone could have thrown himself so deeply into a situation for me; it moved me. A day after that, I received a call from the district hiring manager to do an interview with Ms. Karen Dunlap, the Aventura Mall kiosk manager. Before that interview, I sat down with Ms. Hope to go over the interview and some keywords to say. We did some research on Karen to try to learn about her personality and what she liked and disliked. For that interview, I wore a navy-blue suit and a bright red tie. We spoke for about forty-five minutes on the second floor of the mall in the food court. Once we were done, she told me to have a look at the store and introduced myself to the employees. This time, before I left, she told me that she was impressed by me and would love to have me as part of her team. Inside, I was jumping up and down like Rocky in front of the Philadelphia Museum of Art. I was thinking that I'd finally made it!

A week later, three days before Year Up graduation, I got a call from HR offering me the job. The funny thing is, the other positions I applied for were English speakers, but the one I got was way out of my league. The main customers who come to the store speak Spanish and Portuguese, sometimes a little Russian and French in the winter. Despite the fact that I did not speak Spanish, Portuguese, or Russian, I finished as number one in the store during my first year working there.

That experience taught me that in life sometimes you will get a lot of no's before you get that one yes. These no's can be brutal, and much of the time you will come close to believing the situation is hopeless, but I was able to see that "no" as the NEXT OPPORTUNITY. All the doors that were shut in front of me taught me to persevere and not lose faith. All I needed was only that ONE YES, and everything would change. I am genuinely grateful for people like Mr. Suarez and Ms. Hope who encouraged me to keep applying, to keep going to those interviews. I am indebted to someone like Karen who gave me a shot when many were choosing a safer bet in another candidate.

Graduation:

To tell you the truth, since the day I was accepted into the Year Up program, one of my goals had been to be the student speaker. As fate would have it, I was voted by my peers to be the student speaker for graduation. Once the staff made the announcement, two things came to my mind: "What am I going to say to my peers?" and "How do I encourage Class Two to trust the process when it starts getting challenging?"

I really did not want to blow it. It was the first Year Up graduation, and I was the first student speaker for Year Up South Florida. I wanted my speech to be special because people will always remember it, either good or bad. Inevitably, the pressure was getting to me; my entire family was coming, and my supervisor and his staff were also invited. All our first corporate partners and the organization's CEO, Mr. Gerald Chertavian, and his staff were coming, as were the president of Miami Dade College, Mr. Eduardo Padron, and the campus president. I had been voted to represent the entire class in front of all these people.

I struggled to find the best way to write my speech. Finally, I made the decision to go back to my roots. The best way to express myself was to find a way to talk about my background and graciously thank everyone who had made this moment possible for me and my peers. I also wanted to focus on the future and the responsibilities of the classes that would come after us. I believed that only three words would create that balance:

- Resilience—because the students needed to know that there would be times when they would have to recover quickly from adversity to succeed in the program

- Courage—because they would need to have the backbone to keep going when things got tough,
- Hope because they needed to trust the process and expect that things would work out. It was definitely not going to be easy, I knew that from my own experience, but if a person had these three traits, they would go the extra mile.

One week before graduation, I titled the speech *"I see a beautiful journey that can only be reached by our resilience, courage, and hope."* I rehearsed the speech every night before I went to sleep, making sure that I pronounced and enunciated every word to perfection. I worked on my tone, where I paused, when to emphasize more. I rehearsed so much that I could recite the entire speech without looking at it. Some people thought I was overdoing it, but they could not have been more wrong. I believe that, in life, it is vital to do everything with intent; live on purpose and not half-ass anything.

The day of the graduation, I walked in with my family, two of my best friends, Jude and Jean-Paul, and Elpidia. They were all by my side, as they had been since the beginning. The room was beautifully decorated with balloon arches and garlands of blue and gold. Everyone was professionally dressed, walking around and socializing. The ceremony commenced with the President of Miami-Dade thanking the staff, students, and families for coming. The Year Up staff spoke about the success that Class One had been and presented awards to the staff members who had made it possible. Finally, after weeks of preparation, it was my big moment. I was called on stage. I stood and walked towards the podium. From that moment on, it felt like I was embarking on something much bigger than what I had envisioned.

As I watched the future class, I could not stop thinking about how quickly time had gone by, because it felt as though it was only yesterday I had been in their place attending a Year Up commencement ceremony for the initiation of the program. Now the first year had come and gone, and Class One had actually completed the entire program with full success. I could not help but wonder what type of legacy our pioneer class would leave them. With their eyes on me as I stood on the podium that day, I understood and felt all their hopes and anxieties, all their dreams. That moment revealed to me why I was chosen by my peers to deliver the speech on behalf of the class.

The way forward was clear and focused on the things we really cared about—helping others see how great their future could be, yet advising them that reaching that destination would require focus and hard work. Nothing is given in Year Up; you have to earn it. I took a few seconds to glance around the room, and then I took a deep breath and began...

I see a beautiful journey that can only be reached by our resilience, courage, and hope.

It was resiliency that carried Haiti more than 200 years ago to become the first free black nation on earth; resilience also pushed Dr. Martin Luther King to walk and stand before millions of people to share with boldness his dream for America; that same resiliency embodied Nelson Mandela to not seek his own justice but rather look to unify a divided country.

Ladies and gentlemen, I stand before you today, carried by the same resiliency to tell you, we have made it. It was an uncertain journey—everything we did was new—but we did it. We've set the path; we've lit the torch that symbolizes opportunity. Now, to the class that will come after us, it's time to carry the torch of opportunity to the young people of our generation.

To my peers, despite the negative labels that society has created for us, despite the different names they've called us— lazy, lost generation, dependent—you stood tall and kept moving. We embarked on this journey with the certainty of proving them wrong, with the assurance of changing the life that was written by other people for us, with the determination to bring closure to the opportunity divide that exists among underprivileged young adults. On that journey we knew one thing: when success presents itself overnight, it will surely depart in the morning. However, if we want lifetime happiness, if we want to succeed, we will need to reject all these labels and embrace the failures along the way. For there is no peace without suffering, no rest without strain, no laughter without sadness, no success without failure, and that is what we have to endure as human beings.

To the Year Up staff, thank you will never be enough. Since the beginning, you have instilled in us the value of work, the value in never expecting a handout, to welcome diversity, and to always strive to learn.

To our amazing business partners, we say thank you for the opportunity and the skills we have learned from working at your corporations. The horizon before us is brighter; the challenges of this new generation can and will only be able to be overcome by investing in young adults like us. Since the first day of this program, we knew not to expect a handout, but to work hard to earn it. The same mindset will be transferred to the workplace.

Victor Hugo once said, "There is nothing more powerful than an idea whose time has come." Class 2, I am not trying to give you false hope nor shape an imaginary dream. But it is with great humility and a humble spirit that I am asking you to join me and my peers in a journey where, if your determination is stronger than doubt, if your courage is more resilient than your fear, and you have the audacity to dream a better world for yourself, your family, and your community; then the door of success will be opened wide.

Therefore, I dare all of us to dream, dream big. I could not put these words in a better way than how Og Mandino put them. He said, "So long as there is breath in me, that long I will persist. For now, I know one of the greatest principles of success; if I persist long enough, I will win." Ladies and gentlemen, my question for all of you this morning is, are you persisting long enough?

Thank you!!!

May God bless you, and May God bless this program.

Ten years have lapsed since my graduation from Year Up, and six since the initial publication of this chapter. At time of this re-publication, Year Up South Florida (YUSFL), has served over 1089 young adults. Now, as I pen this update, I find myself enveloped in a profound sense of cyclical journey, a return to the genesis of my transformative experience. Working at Year Up, I've come to realize, is akin to coming full circle, a seamless transition from being a participant to an integral part of the organization.

In my early days as a Year Up participant, the staff's excellence was unmistakable; they were the epitome of dedication and authenticity, tirelessly working to bridge the opportunity divide one student at a time. Their genuine commitment to our growth and success left an indelible mark on me, shaping not just my career but my very core. Now, standing on the other side of this divide, or perhaps more accurately, from within its core, my perspective has deepened, my appreciation for this organization has magnified.

My inaugural year as a staff member felt like a renaissance of my Year Up experience. Being part of the internal dynamics, sitting in meetings where leadership strategies are crafted, listening to conversations brimming with insight and purpose, I've gleaned a deeper understanding of what makes Year Up so unique. Collaborating closely with my colleagues—those newly hired and seasoned employee alike—I've witnessed a shared passion that transcends time and position.

Yet, like any endeavor in life, Year Up is not without its imperfections. But these imperfections are far outweighed by the culture of excellence, the visionary leadership, the unwavering commitment to our mission, and the extraordinary talents of the staff. These elements coalesce to create an environment that, in my experience, comes closest to what one might describe as one of the best organizations in the sector.

In the corridors of Year Up, among the flurry of activities and the hum of purposeful work, I see reflections of my past self in the faces of current participants. Their aspirations, challenges, and triumphs mirror my own journey, reminding me daily of the importance of the work we do. Every success story that emerges from these halls, every barrier dismantled, every bridge built, every life uplifted, serves as a reaffirmation of Year Up's impact.

As I continue to contribute to this remarkable organization, I do so with a heart full of gratitude for the journey that brought me here. It's a journey that began as a participant and continues as an impactor, each day a step in an ongoing story of positive and actionable change.

Chapter 9
BLACK IN AMERICA

I have had several revelations about my experience of living in America. My current life is significantly different than my previous life in Haiti. I tried to blind my thoughts in matters relating to skin color, with the belief that the concentrated emphasis placed on it was an overreaction. I'd even tried to distance myself from being identified solely as a black man and instead as considering myself Haitian, not African-American, and making sure my name is pronounced as *Dahveed* not *David*. My thoughts were that if I were to possess an education, wear proper clothes, and force myself to speak better English, I might escape the discrimination so deeply rooted in American culture.

Remarkably, the birth of my son woke me from a state of slumber and naivety. His entering this world reminded me that he is a person of color, and he will have to face this reality in one way or another. I could no longer ignore the distinctions of race nor distance myself from the unavoidable prevalence of the law of identity so long as my son was breathing and his eyes could gaze upon mine. The law of identity states that an individual is who they see themselves as. With this in mind, I see myself and my son both as men of color. I view us both as free.

I shall commence with the notion of self-esteem in being a person of color. The issue of self-esteem in Haiti stems directly from poverty. This contrasts slightly to the self-esteem issue in Afro-America in that the challenge transcends wealth. That is to say, an individual of color may possess many of the financial accommodations that the nation of America may have to offer but still have a sense of inadequacy, despite the fact. I feel that this may be of transgenerational origin and is inherited. Centuries ago it was not encouraged that a person of color should believe in his or herself. What I observe today is a yearning for many colored people to love themselves. This lack of confidence is seen in Haitian culture as well, but feels more prevalent in the African-American culture. Again, this is merely what I have interpreted from watching and living within both communities thus far

I have also witnessed what I believe to be solidarity between black community members across different African-American communities. This may be mainly due to the fact that there is still a culture of deep mistrust between minorities and government which is still being led by a group of people with underlying discrimination towards others outside of their own race or community. I've noticed that both black and white individuals only find refuge within those communities in which people look like them.During a related conversation, a friend candidly expressed to me that knowing your history is very helpful since it may result in preventing one from making the same mistakes as their forefathers.; However, sometimes knowing too much of your history and holding it too close can be harmful. Holding on to the past can stop someone from moving forward. Instead, one must grow from it. How many times have you heard someone quote history, just to fuel the mistrust he or she might have toward a race, which stops any kind of genuine path towards a better community together? Many times, we refer to not judging a son by the sins of his parents; therefore, the children should not be guilty of the crimes of their ancestors, nor should they carry in perpetuity a generational guilty verdict. Such a mindset only prevents us from creating our own path. By no means am I saying to forget the misdeeds of the generations before us, for there are still some atrocities that reverberate in today's society. Even as I am writing this, more black people are imprisoned than any other race. African-Americans and Black Americans are more prone to face discrimination in the education system, workplace, or justice system. I am certain that by the time this book is published, no laws or policy drastically remedying the situation will have been passed. However, that doesn't mean that to survive, African Americans should only look out for one another.

Coming from Haiti, a black nation, there is no constant reiteration of things "being black" as it is already understood that there are few alternatives outside of an already black majority. That is not to say there is no form of racial discrimination— for example, people in Haiti who cannot speak French are discriminated against constantly. The vast majority of Haitians speak Haitian-Creole, a language birthed from the encounter of French and various African dialects. The government is predominantly French speaking, in which only a small number of citizens in the country are literate. The laws by which the Creole speakers have been governed are solely in French. The best middle schools and high schools in Haiti more often than not encourage students to speak French instead of both languages. This idea has resulted in the exclusion of the majority of the populace from formal political involvement. If one does not speak French, he or she is looked down upon. That is why Haitian parents would rather work around the clock than not be able to afford to send their kids to reputable, French-speaking schools. Like parents everywhere, all Haitian parents want their children to survive discrimination and persevere against the intimidations of being looked down upon for societal factors.

Another aspect where discrimination can be observed in Haiti is colorism. In Haiti, those held in high regard tend to be lighter in skin pigment or biracial. This phenomenon could be argued to be different in the States, since someone of darker skin in America is revered as being more connected to African Heritage. Within African American culture, a lighter pigmented person may often be shamed as one who would be better suited for an "in-house" position back in the days of slavery.

Nonetheless, in Haiti, there would never be a promotion of a "Black-owned business" or any other color, for that matter. In America, many black owned businesses emphasize that they are black owned. The majority of America is still being led by non-Africans, therefore some find that there is incentive for people to shop at black-owned businesses.

Dr. Martin Luther King Jr.'s vision was inclusive. He found a way to make white population better understand the importance of equality without excluding them nor denigrating them. Our goal in this generation ought to be the same. The movement for equality is an important and ongoing one, but I'd argue that the "black lives matter" movement may isolate some would-be supporters since they may not think that they are invited to participate in this particular social change. In my sincerest opinion, the vision is great, but the tactic lacks inclusion and is not a foolproof strategy towards change. As a black person myself, I understand the pain. The urge to say enough is enough. The appetite to disrupt just so people can listen. In the short term it will work, just as we have seen in the past few years since the regrettable death of Trayvon Martin and later on, George Floyd. As you can see now, there are less protests and less noise. These things can work for so long without cooperation from others.

Most of the landmark laws like the Voting Act, Civil Rights Act, and Women Rights Act had participation from other groups. Even the decisions made by the Supreme Court had one or two members from the other ideological spectrum who had crossed over and joined the rest. For instance, Brown v. Board of Education, 1954; Miranda v. Arizona, 1966; Roe v. Wade, 1973. The same thing needs to be done again. There are issues that are human rights, not just black or white rights. The disparities in the sentencing is a human rights issue; the discrimination based on one's skin tone is a human right issue; the overwhelming killing at the hands of the police while the subject is unarmed and present no threat to the officer is a human rights issue. Once color is involved, the public is often coerced into taking a side. When this occurs, no change can be made. We have to learn to win together. Only then can we all respectively have what we seek individually…EQUALITY FOR ALL.

In addition to an unwavering sense of loyalty to blacks by blacks, Haiti is not concerned with expression of African origin as it is a day to day phenomenon which is experienced in nearly all that transpires on the island. There are no pro-black agendas in Haiti because any objective in the lifestyles of the citizens do not leave the confines of enriching the overall Haitian culture. As a matter of fact, there is much more of the contrary. The lighter skinned blacks often hold absolutely no loyalty to other blacks and even less to those who are darker. Fortune takes precedence over the occupancy of black sentiment and racial obligation.

Identity is a crossroad stemming from the past and crossing over to the future. A person can only know who they are if they have a sense of where they have come from as well as where they want to go. Although the past presents the current circumstance that an individual may be in, it does not and should not ever anchor who a person can grow to become. For the most part, Haiti and Afro-America do not have the same ideologies as far as appreciation and pride for their past. In the Haitian culture, there are very few regrets about its past. The same may not be viewed by many of those of the African-American culture. By this, I am suggesting that it is highly less traditional for most African-Americans to lovingly embrace their history here in America. Arguably, Haiti has an exclusive culture expressed in the language, food, music and customs directly transmitted by means of the slave trade. African-American culture in America seems disconnected from African culture.

One thing about African Americans I have always respected is how much discouragement they historically had to have endure. Having never had the opportunity to rebel in America yet still continuously making strides to freedom. The Underground Railroad is the most fascinating story of freedom that I have ever read about. Running way must have required so much determination and hope. African-Americans did not have the luxury of being isolated on an island, therefore their fight for freedom has always been greater than that of other Afro-descendant nations. African-Americans are still in search of social equality in terms of respect. Things have improved astoundingly from the era of lynchings, and then segregation. While progress is certain, it will not occur overnight. The road to equality is long.

I am acutely aware that we have not arrived yet, there is still a lot of work to be done. I have mentioned some earlier to remind you that as a society, America has not stayed stagnant. We might not be where we need to be, but we definitely are not where we used to be. That is why despite what is going on, I am grateful for what this country has allowed me to become.

The American dream is still alive in this generation. I came here with the expectation to be better than my previous self and dare to dream things that are hardly possible anywhere else on this planet. America is still a Beacon for hope and where unlikely dreams can become a reality, and transformations do happen.

America is beautiful and its beauty is expressed in its ability to welcome us all. The strength of this country has always been its ability to be a mosaic of cultures and ideas, allowing you to hold to your values, your culture, and the freedom to have your own faith without any fear of being prosecuted. Although there is a lot to improve upon, these are just a few of the positive reflections I see in this country - things we must not take for granted, but instead things for which we should continue to be grateful.

In late November 2015, the Year Up National Alumni Association started a campaign entitled, "YUMATTER". The campaign aimed to deliver a message to shift the paradigm of images the mainstream media shows of minority youth, and allows them to own the narrative of what it means to be worthy of the responsibility that comes with crossing the opportunity divide. In contribution to that campaign, I wrote a letter to my son, a black kid growing up in America.

Dear Dahveed,

I am writing this letter to you because the end of year is approaching and soon it's going to be Christmas. It's the time when we take a pause, reflect, and ask the deepest questions about our lives. Who are we? How shall we live? What's our role in this current generation?

It's also a time to say thank you to loved ones and people who have played an instrumental part in our life. My son, you are the most important thing that can ever happen to your mom and I, and you will always be our beloved son. You have given us more joy than you can ever know.

Upon that reflection, I couldn't go any further without telling you what I hope my generation leaves for yours. I grew up believing the best things any parents can give to their children are values to live by and an identity so that they know who they are.

Dahveed, in my generation, things have not been the best. I have seen tough times, financial collapse, economic recession, wars, covert racism and the opportunity divide widen out of proportion. People have lost their savings, their jobs, even their homes. State- of-the-art prisons are popping out in every state and county, while students are graduating with hundreds of thousands of dollars in student loans and can't even find a job.

Our society right now teaches us to make decisions that ONLY benefit us at the expense of our neighbor. We are becoming more and more obsessed about remembering the price of things while forgetting the value of things; therefore, most of us forget why we matter; we forget that our voice is the most important weapon we possess. At some point during our life, we slowly but surely accept the picture we have been painted as. We grew up thinking our ideas are not our own. The need to fight for something better is worthless.

My son, no more shall you let such poison ensnare you nor give your mic to someone to describe you, nor give up your pen to someone other than yourself to write your own narrative.

Though all may seem lost, I have regained courage and renewed hope through your eyes. My son, I cannot see into the future in any specific sense, but I do see it brighter and better.

I see the strengthening of democracy, equality for all, the creation of a strong and vibrant economy sustained mainly by young adults like you and hundreds of thousands of Year Up alumni.

I no longer see the opportunity divide that once existed in my generation. Owning a business and employment opportunities are no longer out of reach for people like us.

I see more than 6.7 million young people who are re-connected within their societies. Some become respectful homeowners, teachers, and community leaders, politicians with principles and values, and successful business owners.

I see you and your generation bold enough to own their narrative. You are no longer seen as dependent, lazy, or a political pawn, but a strong and resilient member of your community. A member whose voice can no longer be silenced or ignored.

I see a renaissance of consciousness and the disappearance of GREED. A fairer and kinder way to build a nation that genuinely understands and accepts diversity and where talent comes from.

I see the youth of your generation finally realize their full potential and know they indeed MATTER and fully embrace their roles as change-makers who are vital for the growth of their families and communities.

My son, in you, I see a better world.

Love, your dad.

BLACK IN AMERICA

Chapter 10

HAITI IS NOT DEAD—YET

The media and the NGOs take pride in selling you images of Haiti involving food insecurity, trash, and little kids playing in the dirt. They have an agenda, which is to make money. I have an issue with this narrative, not because it is not true, but because it is incomplete. The country still has hard-working citizens who are not just looking for a handout. They are doing everything they can to make sure their kids go to school and have a decent meal every day. The country has courageous students, just like I did, walking miles to get to school trying to improve their lives; decent families making an honest living; and a hopeful nation that has refused to give up, believing that one day Haiti can and will rise again.

Stories like those of Solange and Lorien, students I spoke to in some of the universities in the capital when I returned to Haiti after eight years, strengthen my belief that Haiti is not dead yet.

SOLANGE:

She has two children; one is eight years old, and the other is six. Instead of sitting at home and not doing anything, Solange decided to start selling grapefruit to make sure her kids had a decent meal to eat at night. After she is done preparing her kids for school, she leaves her house at 6:00 a.m. to set up on the sidewalk. If Solange makes enough during the day, she takes some from it to prepare a meal for her children. If not, she just mixes sugar and water with bread for them. For the kids to study, she lights a candle because she can't afford electricity. While life is getting more expensive and difficult day by day, Solange is happy to go out every day, trying to make the best of it. After all, what would a mom not do for her kids?

LORIEN:

He is thirty-five years old with three kids and one on the way. He has been in the local marketplace since 2012. For him, there is no day off; he works from Sunday through Saturday from 6:00 a.m. to 5:00 p.m. He takes the kamyonet (bus) from Penier to Delmas 95, a trip that can take more than one hour when there is traffic. Lorien was lucky enough to find a place at the local market, which comes at a heavy price for someone like him. Just to sell where he is, he has to pay 2000 HtG per year and 250 HtG per week. Because he works all day, he saves every penny to pay for a tutor for his kids. Unfortunately, at night they still struggle because he can't afford to pay for electricity. In spite of all these financial struggles, Lorien sets up his workplace with gratitude and a good spirit. "My kids are my life," says Lorien while looking at me timidly. Then he put his head down. He continued to say, "Only God can save Haiti; this country is doomed. 'Neg yo twò visye', translated "these politician guys are too greedy". *But if I or my kids have a chance to see a good government, I would like to see the road to Port-de-Paix done and lower the prices of the products we are buying." Can someone really say that Lorien is asking for too much? Should he have to make this choice between paying for food or tutors and electricity for his family?*

Since I emigrated to the United States, I have since returned to Haiti with a desire to listen to the stories of those who live there, and to hear their frustrations and dreams. Whether I was meeting a merchant in the local market or the head of a gasoline pump in Port-au-Prince; whether I was talking to a homeless kid cleaning cars on the street or a student at University Quisqueya in Port-au-Prince, or listening to people who were pro-government or indifferent or hostile to the government, I was respectful. I gently refrained from interrupting and purposely opened my ears to hear what they had to say. I listened to them talk about the lack of jobs, the delayed payment that often lasts up to a year if not more, their struggles to put food on the table, their disdain for the politicians. Most of them, like Lorien, were too busy making ends meet to pay attention to politics, and they talked to me instead about what they were experiencing on a daily basis, wondering where they would find money to pay the next month's rent and their kids' tuition.

I knew the cost of living was very bad; I had grown up with it. But what struck me the most was how low people's hopes were, and how universal that point of view was with every Haitian, no matter their religion, region, or class. They all shared the same beliefs: they wanted employment opportunities for youth and farmers, small merchants, and fishermen, who should enjoy better social recognition of their role in the development of the country; they wanted better pay for teachers and workers, and recognition of the value of their functions; that every children should have access to a quality education and that their parents should not have to be rich to find a spot at one of our universities; and they wanted to ensure that all citizens should have access to basic social services in all communal sections.

That was it. Can anyone really say that they are asking for too much? I do not think so. I refuse to accept the idea that our voices are useless and unable to impact the outcome that is unfolding all around us. I refuse to believe the notion that young Haitians and Haitian Americans do not give a crap about Haiti. I refuse to accept the idea that the same politics we have experienced for so long cannot change and that we are doomed no matter what. I refuse to believe that there are not enough trustworthy, well-equipped, and intellectual Haitians to take the baton and lead the country.

There is clearly a choice we have to make to change the trajectory of the country. Once Toussaint L'Ouverture was arrested and later died in prison, our forefathers also had to make a choice. Would they give up the fight for freedom, or continue to live in slavery? They chose to stand up and fight. In the end, we became the first black nation in the world to gain our freedom. Enslaved people had thrown off their shackles and declared their right to self-determination. When we were occupied by the U.S. from 1915 until 1934, we had to make another choice. Do we fall back and let the memory of Toussaint, the blood of Jean Jacques Dessalines that is flowing through our veins, and the courage of Capoix live only in the history books, or do we regain our true self and fight for the autonomy of our country? The U.S. military often used violence to suppress anyone who opposed foreign occupation. In one confrontation alone the U.S. military killed more than 2,000 Haitian protesters.[8] In spite of all of this, they chose to fight against the occupation. Elections under the occupation were rigged, a treaty was passed by force, martial law was declared, military tribunals were held, the press was censored, the Haitian Senate was dissolved, the constitution was changed by an unconstitutional plebiscite, and opposition was violently repressed.

For nineteen years, the United States controlled customs in Haiti, collected taxes, and ran many governmental institutions with the intent to benefit the United States, not Haiti. Despite all this, Haitians would not give up. It was not in our blood to be occupied by a foreign country. For nineteen years, heroes like Dr. Rosalvo Bobo, Charlemagne Peralte, and many militants from the *caco* rebel group put their lives on the line to oppose the occupation. When we won, that moment was considered our second independence.

When dictators like Francois Duvalier (Papa Doc), his son Jean-Claude Duvalier (Baby Doc), and Jean Bertrand Aristide took power and led the country with an iron fist, they showed no respect for a free press and led with tyranny over the youth. But again, despite

---

[8] http://www.revcom.us/a/456/american-crime-80-1915-1934-haiti-en.html

this suppression, we chose to act, and again our resilience pulled us together. We overcame it.

It is our resilience and our ability to keep going that keeps us standing in spite of slavery, U.S. occupation, dictators like the Duvaliers and Aristide, storms, and earthquakes. It is because of that courage that we have emerged more determined, more steadfast, and more resolved than before.

Today, my generation needs to make a choice. None of us can afford to be on the sidelines and we cannot just observe the situation; nor can we just say, "the Haitian people do not need our help." There is no place for indecisiveness. The survival of the country truly does depend on how involved we choose to be.

We have seen the same old names, the same clans, the same ideologies give birth to the same old politics. We have seen it in the faces of the people who are affected the most; in the farmers, the small merchants, the students, the unemployed youth. It's everywhere.

I'm reminded of a conversation I had with my mom late 2016 about farming, and how farmers used to work together. She used the word *"konbit"*. That word embodies solidarity among the community and empowers us to do everything within our power to better ourselves together. Because if this time around it was my grandfather who needed them, they all knew they could count on him to show up when they needed him as well. My mom, being the only daughter of her father, was not allowed to go on the farm. My grandfather would hire other people to do the light work that was needed; nevertheless, my mom would try to sneak out to go see the workers. Even today, while reflecting on it with me, she still does not fully understand how these workers were able to pick the rice on a straight line without any ruler, to do it fast and for such a long period of time. One thing she believes might have helped was the song they would sing on their way to the rice field and while they were working. Togetherness was at the core of their work, the true meaning of "I am my neighbor's closest family, and we cannot just survive—we can thrive collectively." My mom told me that was the true spirit of the song they would sing:

"Youn fe pou lot, lin sevi lot

Nan pouin ki met, nan pouin k-esklav

S-ou pa travay, mouin p-ape viv

Si-m pa travay, ou p-ape viv" [9]

"Everyone helps each other and serves one another.

We are neither masters nor slaves.

If you don't work, I will not eat.

If I don't work, you will not live."

Their heads bent in the ground bending their backs to pick rice, they would go hours and hours singing this song while working. They were empowered by their labor, motivated to know that out of this land comes dignity, the value of hard work being passed to their kids, and a means to afford an education to better equip their kids to not only become great citizens, but also valuable members in the community. So, if you are lucky enough to hear Haitian singing this song, understand that through this song they are projecting the spirit of togetherness; a *konbit* in its purest form.

---

9   Colimon, Frantz, and Jean Gérard. "Youn fè pou lòt". N-ap réglé tout bagay an chantan. 22 ed. (Ps. 49, 5). Port-au-Prince: 2007.

KONBIT IN ACTION

I saw *konbit* when I was growing up in the country. I saw it when I returned back to Haiti, after eight years, through the stories of Solange and Lorien and the students I spoke to in some of the universities in the capital.

It is as though a select few found the key to the opportunity door, but none of them bothered to share it with everyone else. The rules of the game were changed right under our noses, but no one cared to inform us or give us a hint. If we choose not to act like our forefathers did, the remainder of the country that we hold so dear to our heart will be there no more. The Haitian values to which you always refer will become a mere memory. The pride of a free nation that you are so used to showcasing every January 1 and May 18 and the celebration of the fight on November 18 will be recorded only in the history books and placed on a library shelf somewhere.

So, let us DARE to work together, let us DARE to look for a way to positively contribute to the development of a renewed Haiti. Instead of always returning to what our ancestors did more than 210 years ago, let us DREAM of a better Haiti, one with access to education for all, job opportunities for our professionals, and a decrease in the cost of products for small merchants. I remain fully confident that there is an army of young, dedicated, and professional Haitians who will be willing to lead the country or be part of the solution-driven conversation if the opportunity were to present itself.

Take, for example, Marc Alain Bouccicault, co-founder of Group Echo Haiti, a group that focuses on facilitating the emancipation of Haitian youth while taking actions with significant impact on development in Haiti. From that organization came "Elan Haiti," a project from a series of reflections, lectures, tours, workshops, and round tables then devoted to a profound, sincere, engaged discussion focused on Haiti among young students, active leaders, and Haitian and international entrepreneurs selected competitively in order to promote horizontal exchanges and the necessary dialogue on major national issues, while promoting concrete actions in favor of the positive development of Haiti. With all that, Marc still finds the time to be the coordinating ambassador for Central America & Caribbean at One Young World, an organization that gathers together the brightest young people from around the world, empowering them to make lasting connections to create positive change. Marc is among eight members to bring the biggest tech event to Haiti on June 6–7, 2017. "Haiti Tech Summit," a thirteen-year initiative of the Global Startup Ecosystem, that acts like a digital accelerator into emerging markets.

Another influence in our community today is Makisha Noel. She reminds me of my parents in that, when they have something intimate to share with us, they will always call us in the living room. It is where they shared their most intimate conversations, opened up about their worries, and laid down their visions as well as their hopes. Makisha does just that and more through her organization called The Living Room Project. It is where all conversation is welcome; any opposite views are sought. When we are in the living room, our goals are to be understood as much as to seek to understand. In these times, where everyone is running towards someone who thinks and speaks the same way they do, Living Room Project conversations thrive in the midst of disagreement. Makisha understands that allowing people to deeply disagree without any personal insult can only breed the best ideas or bring forth an intimate conversation true to the organization's name. Knowing that our background might be different, we all share the same human dignity and deserve to be treated with respect and grace even when there is deep disagreement among us.

Like his sister, Makisha, Jefferson Noel, known as Jeff is a dedicated and passionate young leader I am honored to call a friend. While serving as the senator of community relations with the student government at Valencia College, Jeff discovered a dire need for the community to come together and engage in dialogues that matter. His persistent work to bring about societal change through students at the college caused him to imagine a scenario where all members of the community can galvanize and enact powerful change. Jeff's goal with his organization *Barbershop Speaks* s is to provide *Education through Conversation*. During Barbershop Speaks events, he engages in intelligent discussions to enlighten, educate, and empower the community toward a more enriching future. He realized that for a community to shift their paradigm one must reach out to everyday folks in the community and challenge them to think more deeply about old customs and rules. He has held events on political engagement, education, race, financial literacy, and mental health. Through these events, he has been featured on National Public Radio, WLRN, and recognized by Congresswoman Frederica Wilson and the City of Miami. Through Barbershop Speaks, Jeff is transforming local communities, and he will impact cities as well.

I would be remiss if I did not talk about Wanda Tima-Gilles from L'Union Suite. She is the epitome of a dedicated young woman, the reincarnate Sanite Belair or Marie Jeanne Lamartiniere in the flesh living among us once again. Wanda has had to overcome every obstacle thrown at her and has turned the other cheek when being faced with rejection early on just to have her eyes on the prize—a Haiti that can be known for its culture, its people, its history.

These few individuals are just a drop in the bucket full of amazing young leaders leading in their respected fields. They have seen what works, they have experienced a government that cares about its citizens, and they enjoy peace and prosperityF. These people are everywhere, both in Haiti and throughout the world. They are begging for a chance to be part of that change. I call upon all Haitians, specifically young ones, to pay more attention to our homeland, to learn about your story and look for any way to contribute. You still share that blood, and as long as the blood keeps flowing through your veins, Haiti lives on.

What if we are the generation that bridges the gap between the rich and the poor, the Creole speaker and the French one? Envision us holding a true election with the participation of all Haitians, not a selection from a few special groups. What if we are the generation that provides clean water to our brothers and sisters? What if we give our farmers the tools, the education, and the assistance to grow their crops? What if we are the generation of entrepreneurs and businesspeople to create enough jobs for our university students, so they don't feel obligated to risk their life elsewhere? What if we are the ones who build lasting infrastructure in the country—better roads, better bridges, buildings that will last, and more universities? What if instead of dozens of people dying in the sea while trying to escape a hopeless life, they stay because they know that we will buy their products once they produce them?

Imagine us working on solutions that our children will be able to enjoy for years to come.

Those engaging in *konbit* are among us. They do not get a lot of attention, nor do they seek it, but they are busy doing the work this country needs done.

I see them everywhere I travel, in the capital and outside. I see them when I pass our universities and schools. I interviewed some of them weekly for my podcast. I know *you* are there when I see you study for that next exam under the light pole because you do not have electricity at home. You are not the loudest voice in the room, but I see your quiet, sturdy spirit.

I see it in the farmers who keep working the land to make sure the banana, the rice, the mango, and the cacao can produce fruits to keep their businesses open and pay for their kids' tuition even after a natural disaster had just struck their lands and completely destroyed their crops.

I see it in the courageous students who walk five to seven miles to school, who did not eat while coming and going from class. Those same students stay up late to finish their homework, and the teachers, despite not getting paid for the past five months, continue to come to class and teach their students. I see it in the way the teachers put the students' needs ahead of theirs.

I see it in the police officers who put themselves at risk going after gangs and kidnappers to make sure the population can live in peace and security.

I see it, like it or not, in the eyes of the protester determined to prove that injustice can no longer be the norm, that living costs cannot keep skyrocketing. I see it in the young couple who just married, trying to build a life together while thinking about the future of their kids in a country like ours.

I see it in the mother who gives almost everything to send her kids to the university. I see it in the father who was forced to let his daughter live with a stranger in the hopes that, in return, the child would go to school and not fall into child slavery. I see it in the elderly woman who waits in line to cast her vote.

That is the Haiti our forefathers envisioned for us and the one for which they laid down their lives. It is still here. It is in us. No matter where you are, no matter your lifestyle, no matter the country you live in now, no matter your education level. As long as your heart beats with sincerity, you have the power to influence the next human being and even a nation.

That is the Haiti I know; that is the Haiti many of you believe can come about. That is the country we love. That is the full picture you will not find on TV or on those NGOs' websites. Hard working. Courageous. Intelligent. Warm hearted. Hospitable. I am as optimistic as you are and confident about the future because I know that my generation, Haitians and allies, will rise and drive out the darkness that has covered us for so long.

Chapter 11
NEC PLURIBUS IMPAR
HAITI, AN EXPERIENCE LIKE NO OTHER

Hospitality is a relationship between a host and guest. Hospitality involves providing guests with quality services, generosity, and memories that they will always remember. Showing hospitality to people demands a strong load of character and a set of skills, such as communication, customer service, cultural awareness, and language skills. The end goal is ensuring that the guest is delighted with the experience they had so much so that they will return. Yet, if you were to ask the people I met during my trip to Haiti, I believe they will only define hospitality as being the best human being you can be, and treating someone just as you would like to be treated. Nothing more, nothing less.

Customer service is a very important aspect of hospitality. It is necessary to ensure that the guest has a wonderful time throughout his or her stay. Excellent and quality customer service is all about ensuring that the guest expectations are met and the guest leaves happy—happy enough to give good reviews to others. It's what Ralph De La Vega, former Vice Chairman of AT&T Inc and CEO of AT&T Business Solutions, likes to call "Lagniappe" which is to do a little bit extra, go the extra mile to wow the customer. The ability to communicate to guests in their mother tongue will also make the whole experience more enjoyable with the aim of ensuring that the guest feels at home. Being multilingual is a strong asset for demonstrating hospitality to guests. Interacting with guests and addressing their needs is important, and this is where the communication skills come in.

Others will say cultural awareness is also very essential, and it is. However, the hosts, which a majority of them were strangers, just wanted to have an open dialogue, a willingness to be good listeners while simultaneously showcasing their pride for their city and neighborhood.

Understanding and respecting the cultures and behaviors of the guest helps to create a strong bond between the host and the guest, thus fortifying the guest and host relations and making the experience an all-around enjoyable one for the guest. It is also necessary to take into consideration beliefs and values, for these are aspects that represent a person's culture.

Five or ten years ago, I could not have seen myself in such a position, where I am able and fortunate to do local tourism. When I was in Haiti, after every school break, I always receded back to my hometown, Saint-Marc. It never once occurred to me that I should go somewhere other than my home, even if it was for one day, try a different city, meet different people, learn about the culture in the south or the north. These things were too foreign, and I could not afford to be a local tourist either.

Here I am, ten years later, in Port-au-Prince putting my bag in the Terios, making a few calls to my AirBnB host to secure my stay in a city I have heard so much about yet know so little about. In the front of the car is my friend, Moise, who will be driving Francky and I. Francky is my videographer and partner in a project we are doing in Haiti. Moise popped open the hood of the car to check the oil, water, and anything else to make sure we will be able to safely drive through the route many call "Karate Mourn," while others are a bit more dramatic and call it "revenge route." That's how dangerous the route is. It was built by the French, thus the reason for such a name.

With the key in the ignition, we were on our way to Jacmel, I looked at my watch to see how long the drive would take. It was 10:00 a.m. I have never been farther south than Port-au-Prince and did not know what to expect, but I was curious to drive through "Mourn

Karate." I'd been warned by my driver and even strongly advised to take a pill to sleep in order to not react while driving through there. Lo and behold, I was taken aback when I looked through my sideview mirror and saw the route we just passed and all the curves left in front of us. It was like a coiled snake. I kept thinking about the Daihatsu Terios we were driving in. Was it well maintained? When was the last service done? Was the person who did the service certified to do so? All these questions seemed to come to mind a bit too late. I had one choice by then: keep my eyes straight ahead and pray that I made it to that city so many coveted.

Eventually, we made it. The big iron decorated "door" on it was inscribed, "Welcome to Jacmel." It was 3:15 p.m. by then.

Jacmel is arguably the most visited city in Haiti besides the capital Port-Au-Prince. It is known by many as the City of Light, mainly because it was the first city to have electricity in the Caribbean. I have yet to meet a Jacmelian who is not quick to thoroughly and proudly inform someone of their background. For them, talking about the city is effortless. It is renowned for its vibrant arts and handicrafts, fresh seafood, and some of the most pristine beaches in the Caribbean, in even the world. It's also known for its enchanting architecture, with top-of-the-line materials straight from the dazzling French castles. I was almost ashamed that I had never been to this part of the country before. This time, I zealously kept a promise I'd made to myself during my Haiti tour that Jacmel would be the first city I'd visit. No one was going to prevent me from visiting Magnifique Yaquimel.

LAKAY

As fate would have it, I received a generous and exclusive treatment when I visited the vivacious cities of Jacmel, Cap Haitian, and Gonaives, among other equally striking cities. This glittering experience is one that I will always remember and share with people I meet on this road we call life. My resilient brothers and sisters have not lost their bona fide welcoming spirit. During my tour of Jacmel, I was fortunate to experience it firsthand. The jovial locals eagerly opened their doors to invite us into their homes and spoke freely about the history of the city and what brought them to Jacmel. For instance, the owner of Hotel Le Florita, Mr. Joe Cross, wistfully told us that it was the insatiable beauty and a seducing culture of the city that stole his heart, and from that point on he knew at the very least he had to buy a residence in the city during his time away from home. I was lucky enough to get a tour of the hotel, which has recently been dedicated as one of the landmarks in the city by UNESCO and ISPAN (Institut de Sauvegarde du Patrimoine National). The Institute for Protection of the National Patrimony was created by decree on March 29, 1979. Its mission is to draw up inventories of real estate of high cultural value; to carry out studies and carry out specific projects of protection, restoration, and development; and to promote public or private activities aimed at the conservation of the national heritage.

For a hotel that was constructed in 1888, I was surprised to find that most of its rooms are intact. Unfortunately, the 2010 earthquake damaged part of the building. Standing from the second floor, Mr. Cross showed my team and me the two stairs—the one on my left, used by the masters, and the other on my right, used by the slaves—because it was unsuitable to have masters and slaves use the same staircase. The bigger surprise was the rooms themselves, significantly unchanged, pristine for a place that old. The same architecture of the nineteenth century, the details used in the ceiling, and the high bed. He even gave us a small joke or a better suited version of why they would have made a bed that high. The dress the lady would have worn would be so difficult to remove that it was easier for the master to have her holding the side of the bed and raise her robe for some quick sex to save time. The room design was also made to allow fresh air to come inside since there was no A/C back then, a design that still works in today's society.

For Williams, another resident living in the city, it was the warmhearted people that made him fall in love with the city. At one point, he told his wife, then girlfriend, that Jacmel would be the final test to see if they were meant to be together. If she did not like the city, then they could not be together. From that moment up to now, they have raised their children in Jacmel and saw the town from its highest point to its lowest, with the ghastly fire in 1934 and the catastrophic earthquake in 2010 that almost entirely destroyed the renowned city. For the natives, it's the eternal calmness of Jacmel that kept them there.

The locals were so welcoming that part of me thought they were just the exception. I kept thinking to myself that I was just lucky to meet so many Jacmelians who believed in community and togetherness.

On our way to the prominent Fort-Ogé, another landmark in the city hidden at the top of Jacmel mountain, my team and I met a young girl who was waiting for a motorcycle taxi to go home. As luck would have it, it happened to be raining, and on top of that, we did not know the way to the fort. We stopped to ask for directions. Luckily, she realized that we were heading in the same direction she was going. Naturally, we gave her a ride, but she kindly decided not to get off when we reached her house and decided to continue with us just to make sure we made it to the fort. Additionally, she knew the group of people in charge of the fort and those who had the key to open the gate. That was fate in its purest form. When we finally arrived at Fort-Ogé, which is named after the dauntless mulatto leader, Vincent Ogé, who led an unsuccessful insurrection against the French in 1790 but instilled in the slaves' minds that they could be free if they dared to fight the oppressors. A year after, the adamant horn of independence rang in every ear of slaves around the globe like the thunderous cry of a mother giving birth to a child, which simultaneously was the lightening of fear that shook the hearts of every oppressor. The fort has impressive rampart walls with a couple of watchtowers and a wide lush courtyard. Unfortunately, it was suddenly brought to a halt due to Dessalines's death in 1806. Nonetheless, the fort still offers one of the best views to see all across Jacmel. I also met Jeanne, an engaging university student who lives next to the fort. She was on her way to an English group study, and she pleasantly stopped and practiced English with me before happily continuing on her way to the group.

After a long day filming and recording on Lakou New York, a main road in Jacmel, fixing our rental car that had been damaged from our trip to the Fort Ogé site, and a second visit to that same site via motor taxi, to say that we were tired is an understatement. So, when we got to our AirBnB we thrust open the door and sprinted in eagerly, dumping our equipment bags on the floor, and jumped on the beds. Like all the other days, we had come back to the house just in time. The night was only just getting underway, and Moise and I were more than excited to get a taste of what it had to offer.

That is when the idea to film the nightlife came. We had done everything else besides taking a shot in the dark in a club to get a sense of how the Jacmelian put it down at night. That was quickly shot down by Moise. "Not tonight, please spare me this. We have been filming all day for two days in a row. Can we just have some fun? I just cannot see you guys go in there with your camera on people's faces. If you want to do it, please count me out. I will not drive you there."

I turned to Francky and said, "He made a fair point..."

"Of course, I did. We should have some fun also," Moise quickly interrupted. Francky looked at him powerlessly and shrugged to show his approval. Francky and I agreed to go as observers, not participants, but maybe we might schedule the owner for an interview about the place.

So we freshened up and changed our clothes. No hesitation. No messing around. We headed for the club and could not wait to get there. That night was about partying and going crazy, so we opted for some beer. We watched people dancing and talking. The dancing got more intense as the compas music got louder and louder until I could not even hear myself. After a quick ride into the district, we wandered around the streets thinking where we should go and what we should do. We settled on one of the most popular spots in Jacmel: Congo Club.

That place was first recommended to us by Fredeline, a waitress we met when we were eating earlier in the day at the restaurant. We drove by two or three times before we finally got a parking space.

"At last!" said Baschemir, Francky's cousin. Moise turned off the car and turned his head and said, "Please, I beg you guys, enough with the interviews. Let us just have some fun, drink a bit. We have worked hard all week, we deserve it."

"OK, sure!" we all replied, but I was already crossing the street.

We made our way in and claimed a couple of seats at the bar, ordering four bottles of Prestige beer, one for each one of us. At the same time, we warned Moise to not drink too much because we had family waiting for us back home in Miami. The moment Moise got his second drink, he downed it in a few minutes and began scanning the room eagerly. "Fredeline was spot on. Look at this place, the music, and all these people dancing compas," Moise said as he looked on excitedly. Compass is a popular music from Haiti. It is dance music and modern meringue with European and African roots.

Already the combination of prestige and fatigue was starting to make me feel spaced out, and pretty soon I was going to get that awesome buzz where I would be pounding but I would be so alive all at once. Before the urge to do something crazy and regrettable kicked in, I told Francky we'd better get going since we had a long day in front of us. Without hesitation, Francky nodded and tapped Moise and his cousin, as if someone who was just waiting for the signal because he himself was visibly tired from all the back and forth with his camera filming and photographing my interviews.

NEC PLURIBUS IMPAR HAITI, AN EXPERIENCE LIKE NO OTHER

Another Jacmel beauty difficult for me to ignore was Bassin Bleu. That place stands head and shoulders above any other tourist attraction in the south region, and in my opinion, should stand toe to toe with Citadel—hat is how beautiful that place is. On your way to the main basin, there are two other basins. The first one is Bassin Yes, named after someone that used to be called Yes. To get to that basin, you just need to cross the rushing river over a series of flat stepping stones where locals in the area will bring their horses to drink some water or wash their clothes. The next basin is Bassin Palmist, because there is a palm tree next to it. That pool itself is impressive and beautiful. However, my view was quickly changed when the tour guide informed me that there is yet another pool to see. Its name was Claire, the French word for "clear." That water leading to that pool is so beautiful and clear that if a quarter fell in the shallow water, you could quickly and easily spot it. And in the deeper waters of the basin, which measured about 75 feet, the water is a true blue. It's a wide and deep pool of turquoise bound by sheer cliffs and huge boulders worn smooth by the passage of water.

Even though I do not know how to swim, I was pulled in by the sheer magnificence of the place and felt compelled to jump into the water. It was a risk I had to take because I felt that I could not cheat myself out of an experience like this one. Luckily, a jumper stood by ready to follow me the moment I went in the water and was able to bring me back to safety. That's an experience South Beach or Laguna Beach simply cannot give you, no matter how popular they are!

A huge thank you to all Jacmelians for your true hospitality, patience, passion, and dedication toward the city and us. You opened your homes to share some of the captivating history of Jacmel with us. Thank you to all our amazing tour guides in Fort-Ogé, Bassin Bleu, Lakou New York, Rue du Commerce, the Marigo Port, etc. Thank you to all the talented artists in FOSAJ. I have met some of the most intelligent and creative environmental activists and many more astounding groups of people. The food was truly mouth-watering, some of the best I have had to this day.

I am humbled and empowered to see the work of the artisans and their passion to work day in and day out to make Jacmel the City of Light in different issues facing the community. Jacmelians in and out of the city, you should be proud of your incredible city.

None of these people knew me or anyone else on my team, but they took the time to converse, assistor laugh with us, and did so with such grace and happiness. And in case you might think that this form of gracious hospitality is simply a Jacmelian thing, it is not. I was welcomed that same way in cities across Haiti, from Cap Haitian and Gonaives.

LAKAY

NEC PLURIBUS IMPAR HAITI, AN EXPERIENCE LIKE NO OTHER

TRAVEL TO CAP HAITIAN

Like Jacmel, it was my first time going to Cap Haitian. I only now have friends from the United States with a connection to that city. When I was heading to Cap Haitian, already in the station waiting for my bus to depart, I messaged a friend on Facebook, Fevry. I told him that I was going to his city, and asked if he could find a place for me to stay for the night. With less than twelve hours' notice, there I was hoping for my friend to come through. My friend messaged me back in under five minutes and told me his childhood friend, whom he considers as a brother, was expecting my call.

When I called, Fevry's friend, Audry, thought I was coming in a week or so. However, when he found out that I was on my way already, he quickly called his manager and requested the next day off just to be available to accommodate my stay and show me the city. If that was not enough, he drove one hour to the station and waited two hours with his girlfriend and daughter in a lightless street in his car before my bus arrived around 8:00, after having left Port-au-Prince at 1:30 p.m. If Jacmel was an artistic and friendly town, I think it is only fitting to call the north the region of hospitality.

That same night, he drove me around the city, and the next day, early in the morning, he accompanied me to the cathedral, Sans Souci Palace, the Citadelle, and more. Then he brought me to Fort Liberte to check out his city. If that's not the pinnacle of hospitality, then I do not know what is. We started the journey as strangers and ended it as family. Thank you, Fevry Pierre, and thank you, Audry.

I would be remiss if I did not mention Gonaives, the City of Independence, where I got a similarly sincere welcome. Gonaives is a city that is at Haiti's every turning point. On New Year's Day in 1804, Dessalines, Christophe, and Pétion signed the Act of Independence that gave birth to the first and only successful slave revolution. In 1985, the city played a pivotal role that ultimately ended the dictator rule of Jean-Claude Duvalier (Baby Doc). Yet again, Gonaives was brought to the spotlight in 2004 after the death of Amiot Mettayer, known by many as Ti Cubain, the leader of a gang group in Raboto that changed the political game and put an end to former President Aristide's second term.

I went through a lot of emotions during my short visit. The first place I went was the independence memorial, the exact place where the Act of Independence was signed. The pride in our tour guide's eyes and the excitement in which he spoke was so touching, and I was fortunate enough to experience it along with students from a local school in the city. They had so many questions and took such pride in the achievement of their forefathers, but the tour guide wisely reminded them it was overdue for our generation to start working on some great achievements of our own. Such a simple request caught me off guard, but he was right. For far too long, we have been enjoying the fruits of our ancestors' achievements.

To end that night in Gonaives, I witnessed the city's employees, under the leadership of the recent mayor, adding back the statue of Toussaint Louverture, which was destroyed due to Hurricane Jeanne. What a moment that was to have witnessed! It could have occurred on any other night, but it just so happened to be that night I was in town for the first time. That experience was mind blowing. To read it on paper or learn it in a classroom that we are the first independent black country is very different than being in the city where the fate of the masters was sealed. I just imagined my forefathers were right there more than 200 years ago to be their own men. It made me stand a bit taller, and I took a moment to recognize the blood flowing through my veins is of them, a perpetual memorial and acknowledgment to their heroic achievement that no one can ever take from me, from us. I know who I am, and I value my past.

However, my most memorable moment in that city was at Petion, where I met a huge cluster of students who were noisily studying in the public place because they did not have electricity at home and had an exam or homework due the next day. I calmly sat in between two of the students who were studying. Roody was on my left studying economics, and Joseph was on my right was studying Haitian Literature. Like many other youths in the country, they truly believe education is not just a key to succeeding, but the only key to make it out and better their lives and their families.

I spent two weeks in Haiti, only three days in an AirBnB and the rest with family and strangers who later became as close as cousins to me. That is how Haiti is, that is how my people are, that is how truly pleasant your visit can be. "NEC PLURIBUS IMPAR" (A nul autre pareil). Indeed, it was an experience like no other. The Haitian people's desire to showcase the unparalleled beauty, the boundless strength, and insatiable taste of our culture is limitless. I'm honored that we are on this journey together.

Hospitality is what made my visit to these wonderful cities a memorable and enjoyable experience, one I will live to remember forever.

Chapter 12

LOST IN TRANSIT: STRANDED BETWEEN WORLDS

Like countless Haitian immigrants before me, I grapple with a profound and complex dilemma—the reluctance to renounce my Haitian citizenship. This hesitation is not merely rooted in the hypothetical ambition of one day running for office in Haiti, but stemmed rather from a deep-seated understanding that my Haitian heritage is an integral part of my identity, intricately woven into the very fabric of my being. My citizenship was not simply a legal status; it represented a badge of honor, a tangible manifestation of my connection to Haiti's rich history and its vibrant, dynamic culture.

Haiti is not merely the land of my birth. It is the place where my ancestors waged valiant battles for their freedom, undeterred by the formidable forces that sought to oppress them. It is the crucible that forged my values of perseverance, hope, and resilience. These values have not only shaped me as a person, but have also guided me to navigate the complexities of life as an immigrant.

To be Haitian is to carry the weight of history, to bear the responsibility of continuing the legacy of our future children, and to hold dear the ideals that have been passed down through generations. It is to embrace the beauty of our culture, the richness of our traditions, and the strength of our people. In the fabric of my identity, the threads of my Haitian heritage are not just mere strands; they are the very warp and weft that give shape and substance to the tapestry of my life.

It was this foundation that fueled my passion for storytelling, culture, and travel, propelling me to explore the world beyond the shores of Haiti. As a flight attendant for a major airline between 2018 to 2022, I had the privilege of visiting over 30 countries, immersing myself in new cultures, and forging connections with countless strangers. Each encounter, each experience, was a thread that added to the rich tapestry of my life. I would love to talk about my first time in Barcelona, the vibrant energy of Buenos Aires, or the timeless beauty of Paris, but this flight to Quito marked me for a different reason.

It was on a picturesque Miami day, the sky a brilliant shade of blue, the fluffy white clouds dotting the horizon. I walked through the airport terminal, the smell of freshly brewed coffee wafting from the cafe by gate 26. Some people were running to their gates, leaving their little ones behind, while others walked calmly to layover flights with time to spare as I made my way to my flight..

I've been granted the opportunity to visit Quito, Ecuador many times through my job as a flight attendant, and it has quickly become one of my favorite destinations. There's something about the city's rich history and hospitable culture that draws me in. This particular time, however, the trip was different. As I arrived at the gate, I noticed a passenger was too sick to fly. Her mother insisted that she was fine, and had already flown from New Jersey to Miami earlier that day. She wanted her daughter to see their homeland once again before she died. At that moment, I understood the passenger's need to connect with her roots, to lay in the soil of her birthplace and feel the ground beneath her one last time. It was a desire I knew all too well.

The lead flight attendant had taken preemptive measures to review emergency onboard procedures, and sure enough, right in the middle of the flight, the sick passenger collapsed. "Code Red - Code Red!" The call went out for a physician on board to assist. The number two flight attendant didn't hesitate; she jumped into action, and let her training take over. The number one flight attendant communicated with the passengers, the pilots, and rest of the staff while I ran to grab any equipment my colleague needed. The number four flight attendant kept a watchful eye on the cabin. As the number two flight attendant performed CPR, the sick passenger's rib cracked, but she continued on. Another rib cracked, and still, she pressed on. Despite our best efforts, the passenger remained unconscious and not breathing. We didn't have the authority to declare her dead, but we knew we had lost her.

In the midst of all this chaos, a passenger in row 1F began hyperventilating, as did the mother of the deceased passenger. As if things couldn't get any worse, the number two flight attendant collapsed unconscious just as we touched down at Quito airport. With one less crew member, we couldn't fly back to Miami that night. We were forced to stay overnight. Unbeknown to me, this would be just the beginning of a nightmare. A trip from hell.

The return flight was canceled, and to my shock and horror, I was denied entry to Ecuador because I did not have a visa. In all my time traveling for work to Ecuador, I had never needed one, and it had never been an issue. This time, the immigration officials offered me two choices: wait in a holding cell with others who had entered the country illegally, or return to the gate and wait six hours for the next flight out. I was stunned. I had done my job, and now I was being treated like a criminal.

As I sat in a foreign land, the fatigue from the long flight weighed heavily on my body. Every store in the terminal had already closed, and the once bustling atmosphere now replaced with an eerie silence. I was trapped in the liminal space of the airport, my stomach growling in hunger without the means to satiate it. The chairs at the gate offered no comfort, their hard surface digging into my back and thighs. My body ached, not just from the physical discomfort but also from the anxiety and fear of the unknown. I tried to close my eyes and rest, but sleep eluded me, my mind racing with thoughts of what lay ahead. I felt the sting of humiliation and anger, the hours earlier of white-glove customer service seemingly forgotten as I was treated like an unwelcome illegal immigrant. I had devoted almost five years of my life to providing the best service possible as a Flight Attendant. Now, I was left stranded, helpless, and alone in a foreign land with no one to turn to. The feeling of betrayal was palpable, and I felt a surge of anger and indignation rise within me. It was at that moment that I decided to apply for U.S. citizenship. It was a difficult choice, but I knew that it was the right one.

A few months later, as I stood in a crowded room, hand raised, taking the oath of allegiance to the United States of America, I knew I had made the right decision. My Haitian citizenship would always be a part of me, a part of my story, but now I was also a citizen of the United States, with all the rights and responsibilities that came with that status.

Reflecting on my journey, I realize that Haiti will always be within me. It is the foundation upon which I have built my life, and it will always be a part of who I am. But I am also grateful to the United States, my adopted home, for the opportunities it has given me and the person it has helped me become.

Chapter 13

LEADING WITH DISTINCTION

Time and change are two important aspects of life. Chronos time will keep existing whether we like it or not. The clock will continue to tick with or without you. Seconds, minutes, hours, days, months, and years will continue to pass. With moving time comes change, and change in various spheres of our lives is inevitable. Most of us detest change because of the unexpected outcomes it brings. To avoid the shock of change, we must utilize the limited time that we have in our hands wisely. Planning is the bridge between time and change. We cannot control the future, but we can influence it with our plans and actions today.

The ability to plan properly is what some leaders in Haiti are missing. Since the early age of our nation, we have fought to overthrow and then replace, but not setting up long-term strategy for the betterment of our people. Those in power in Haiti content themselves with making a change that keeps people at bay and disguises our true intent, which is to stay in power at all costs. However, the void the people tried to rid themselves of remains present and is painfully visible in their faces. To lead without planning is risky; it can be fatal. If you do not know where you are going, every road is the right one—even the one that is worse than the one you were just fighting against.

To avoid such a scenario and secure the future for coming generations, leaders need to be strategic planners and team builders. Haiti needs to strategize a succession plan for its future leaders. This will eliminate coup d'états and their devastating consequences that the country has experienced over the years. The necessity of having a succession plan was articulated in the most profound way by Jesus Christ. He consistently reminded his disciples that He would not always be with them. He encouraged them to learn from Him and lead with courage so that when He left, they would be able to take the ministry forward.

Values of true leadership need to be impressed into the hearts of future leaders of Haiti. They are the ones who will bring the change we desire. They should be molded to become the exact opposite of the current crop of leaders. The true meaning of leadership can be learned from the way Jesus led His disciples and anyone else who followed Him. He emphasized and practiced servant leadership. The Bible recounts the story when His disciples were fighting over who among them would be the greatest. Jesus did not pick anyone but reminded them that it is the kings of the Gentiles who exercise lordship over their people. He told the disciples that he did not wish to see them act as superfluous leaders. Rather, he told them that the greatest among them is whoever is willing to serve others. Jesus revealed to the disciples that leadership, in its essence, is service. People do not become meaningful leaders or lead with distinction without *serving* those that they lead.

The success of any institution depends on its leadership. Leaders are directly responsible for the failure or success of the institutions they lead. The institution can be a family, the church, a school, a company, or a country. Jesus is considered the greatest leader in human history. He saw his role as that of a servant. This is the reason why Christianity has been so successful. With Jesus, His disciples were always first, while He was last. The King of Kings was willing to wash the feet of His followers. Humility was the center of his leadership. He was not afraid to associate Himself with the group of people that the society had rejected: tax collectors and sinners (Mathew 9:9–13); the Samaritan woman (John 4:7–9); and the adulterous woman (John 7).

Had our leaders been compassionate, the problem of refugees from Haiti might have been solved. But as it is currently, people continue to suffer in tents while the leaders who are supposed to help them have turned their backs on them. On the contrary, Jesus demonstrated that a leader needs to be compassionate. Compassion was one of the main pillars of His leadership. In the gospel of Matthew, it is written that when Jesus saw the multitudes, and the way the people were weary and scattered, like sheep without shepherds, He was moved with compassion (Matthew 9:36). We need leaders like Jesus who can sympathize with the millions of people who are suffering in our country, because only they can take the necessary action needed to save the people, and see eye to eye with the people they save.

Despite the numerous challenges, there is still hope for us Haitians. All is not lost. Our leaders must look optimistically into the uncertainty and the chaos. Most importantly, he or she should see both sides – the bright side and the dark side – and having seen both sides, be strong and grounded to make sometimes the hardest and right choice. They never give up hope. However, the kind of optimism that is hereby advocated for should not be blind optimism. They should not be a person who asserts that all is well, when their assertion is contradicted daily by the experience of their citizens. They should aspire to be like Jesus who saw the world as it was: evil and dark.

Jesus led by personal ministering to other people and tending to their needs while putting his own on the back burner. He led by putting himself in the position of a servant while raising others up. In the gospel of Mark, He asked His disciples how long He had to stay with them in order for them to learn (Mark 9:19). He was challenging the disciples to come out of their comfort zone and perform miracles themselves because they also possessed that power.

Lastly, leaders need to use their time in service wisely, and when it is time to leave, they should leave with honor. I started by saying that change is inevitable; therefore, people should not resist it. We know that Jesus told His disciples that it was to their own advantage that He was going away, so that He could send an advocate to them. Without going away, the advocate would not be sent (John 7). He understood that unless he took a step back and let the disciples take a step up, they would never reach their potential. They would always rely on him. That is the mind process of a stretcher leader; they know you cannot grow if they do not stretch you, and the organization cannot reach its full capacity. It might be a good thing to think of the leader holding his followers' hands; they are in a safe and secure position, but sometimes we cannot develop if we are in a comfortable position. Being uncomfortable pushes us to evolve into a better individual, father, mother, son, daughter, and, ultimately, a better leader. So, I want you to know that everything rises and falls on leadership. By looking at Jesus' leadership style, we understand the true meaning of a servant and why we need to approach leadership that way.

Mentoring

Amid all the challenges facing my compatriots in Haiti, I believe that there is still hope for a brighter future. To make sure that the mistakes of our past and present leaders are not repeated, we need to invest in developing the desirable leadership qualities in our youth as demonstrated by Christ. If they grow with a serving mentality, then whether they become parents, church leaders, football coaches, or heads of state, they will understand what leadership really means. They will not be hungry for power; instead they will dedicate their lives to serve others diligently. Such qualities come with the right kind of mentoring. Mentoring takes a long time. It focuses on developing the individual holistically for the future.[10] The youth need to be mentored professionally, personally, and, most importantly, spiritually.

The essence of leadership is service. Leadership is not about holding onto your position for as long as you can. Unfortunately, this is a common practice among our leaders today, as well as the leaders before them. They are afraid to leave their positions. Whenever they hear of a younger person with better leadership qualities, they get scared and look for ways to choke his ambition. These are the kinds of leaders who exercise authoritative leadership as opposed to servant leadership. Good leaders need not shy away from mentoring young people who will one day take their position. According to Dr. Myles Munroe, "The first act of true leaders is identifying their replacement and beginning to mentor them."[11] That is the road to building a lasting legacy as a leader. The leader becomes great by reproducing people greater than himself. That is what legacy is all about.

Christ demonstrated the aspect of leadership development and replacement. He very purposefully prepared the disciples to take over the ministry.[12] We have seen and heard of stretcher leaders in history who mentored others to later succeed them in their works. Socrates mentored Aristotle and Plato, who became the very foundation of Western philosophy and science. Gandhi had Dadabahi Naoroji,

---

10   Thresette Briggs, "Developing Future Leaders with Mentoring and Coaching," Association for Developing Talent blog past (July 2, 2013). Retrieved from https://www.td.org/Publications/Blogs/Management-Blog/2013/07/Developing-Future-Leaders-with-Mentoring-and-Coaching.

11   Myles Munroe, "Passing the Baton of Legacy" (Feb 28, 2014). Retrieved from https://www.youtube.com/watch?v=H49xWwZ7Qzs&feature=youtu.be

12   Ron Edmondson, "12 Leadership Principles of Jesus" (September 28, 2016). Retrieved from http://www.ronedmondson.com/2016/09/12-leadership-principles-of-jesus.html

who became the preeminent leader of the Indian independence movement and the architect of the nonviolence movement. Also, Howard Thurman, Bayard Rustin, and Benjamin Mays mentored Dr. Martin Luther King Jr., who went on to become the leader of the Civil Rights Movement. In the book, *Voices of Women Community College Presidents* authored by Kristen Jones, Kathryn Mueller summarizes the importance of mentorship very well. She says, "If you are standing on someone's shoulders, you need to provide another set of shoulders for the next group. That is a professional and a personal obligation."[13]

So, as a leader, it's imperative to be mindful of other people. In a speech addressing an audience in Montgomery back in 1957, Martin Luther King said, "Life's most persistent and urgent question is, 'What are you doing for others?'" My question is no different today. What are we doing to stretch someone else? What are you doing to develop the next big leader for the country? If you consider the people I mentioned, all of them made an indelible impact in the world in one way or another. Christianity, at its core, is Jesus Christ. A philosopher cannot talk without mentioning Socrates, Aristotle, and Plato; one cannot make reference to the history of nonviolence without acknowledging Gandhi; and one cannot consider the Civil Rights Movement and not recognize the role Dr. King played in it.

Therefore, as it stands, change and time are inevitable in life. Change will happen whether you want it to or not, and time will continue either with you or without you. Dr. Myles Monroe asserts that, at some point, the person who is in a leadership position needs to start thinking about passing the baton to the next generation.[14] They

---

13   Jones, Kristen (2008). *Spiritual leadership: Voices of women community college presidents.*

14   Myles Munroe, "Passing the Baton of Legacy" (Feb 28, 2014). Retrieved from https://www.youtube.com/watch?v=H49xWwZ7Qzs&feature=youtu.be

should not hold on to the throne until they are buried with it because they are afraid of change, or because they fear that their legacy will be lost.

Mentoring is what will ensure that your legacy is sealed. It is dangerous for a company or a government to lead without making a proper plan regarding who will follow once the leader is gone. That is one of the major issues Haiti has faced since the beginning of its existence. The person in power leads without a proper plan, and the opposition does the same thing. We are taught to be dependent, so when we step into a leadership position, we feel insecure and unsure of what to do. We abuse it. We have a sense of fear that if we teach someone what we know or if we have a mentee, that person will take our position. And, in reality, they are supposed to do that. One is doing a disservice to their legacy by not mentoring someone to continue their work. We hide things, make people dependent so that they always come to us. That is a "shrinker" leadership perspective.

Such leaders believe that they are one of a kind; therefore, everyone else is supposed to listen to them and them only. They feel that other people will never accomplish great things without them being in the room. They want to be the source of every "awesome" idea because they consider others as simply inadequate. However, what they fail to realize is that they are killing greater ideas and shrinking people's ability to step forward because they expect their ideas to be not important enough to impact others. In the end, what do the members of a team like this do? They keep quiet and do just the minimum.

Remember what Jesus told his disciples: "It's better for you that I leave." That's the mindset of a "stretcher." They push you to think for yourself. People get smarter when they are together and ideas flourish in their midst because they know they can use more people in the room. Instead of thinking that without them nothing can be done, they trust their teams enough to know that other leaders will emerge and figure out the solution to the problem. For them, it is better that they leave.

So, if you know that time and change are certain, why not plan for a successor? What good does it do to die with your knowledge and experiences? It serves no one, does it? However, that is what you see in the country. You see the same old names doing the same old things, either in terms of women's rights, teachers' unions, human rights, and political parties. I have yet to see someone present a mentee or an assistant. If that person does have an assistant, they try to hide information as much as possible so as to always be needed. However, the moment the boss is not around, the assistant is making moves just to show that they are in control. In the end, you have a power struggle when it was supposed to be an opportunity to mentor someone and a chance for the mentee to learn.

By reshaping the mindset of young people, we will have a great opportunity to teach them what leadership is all about. We can remind them that the best way to leave a legacy behind is to invest in other people. If we begin mentoring young people starting from the last two years of high school and their first year in university and help them develop their leadership skills, the country will be in a much better place because these young people will know what it means to lead. The good thing about a servant leadership approach is that everyone is part of the team working for the same end. It empowers members to play a more critical role in the organization and to be more open to giving and receiving feedback.

THE POWER OF SANT LA

The kind of program that came to mind is the one Sant La is doing. For those who have never had a chance to hear what the Sant La Fellowship is about, it is a community leadership fellowship program that targets Haitian-Americans in South Florida. Young leaders who have demonstrated a passion for volunteering and community involvement. The 12-month program deepens their understanding of ethical and efficient leadership, community-building, Haitian cultural heritage, civic participation, philanthropy, and it will connect them with leaders heading vital Haitian and countywide organizations for the dual purposes of mentoring and creating lasting relationships.

My journey through the fellowship has been an incredible one. I learned a lot about my community in the U.S., especially in South Florida. Throughout this period, I was very fortunate to have met and listened to various Impactors of the previous and current generations. I was humbled by what the generation before us have accomplished in our community, and for them I have found a new admiration within me. The most memorable moment for me and many of my colleagues in the program was the trip we took to Cap Haitian, Haiti towards the end of the fellowship. The founder of Sant La, Ms. Gepsie Metellus, said it best upon sharing her reflection with the rest of the group: "A visit like the Citadel and Palais sans Souci is a trip every Haitians in Haiti and abroad need to take at least once in their lifetime." One can truly understand the meaning of such a statement only by being on the ground and beholding these sights. I fully grasped it myself while I was at the top of Palais Sans-Souci, overlooking the courtyard and part of the Cap Haitian. I quickly realized that even though I had traveled the south and now the north. I finally found myself, at this point in time, standing there admiring what my ancestors had achieved. Literally, I was at the edge of the world, where giants had fallen and unlikely heroes had risen. I experienced a feeling that I have traveled through my history and back to bring the good news— we shall be free again.

While the trip to Haiti might have been the highlight of the fellowship for me, some other major aspects of the program were the labs we attended each month. The discussions were raw and authentic. All of our guests were either the leader of their fields in the community or fully equipped and experienced to ensure we learned as much as we could during the interaction; subjects varied from immigration, education, health care, community involvement, finance, media, ect. The goal was the same: to educate, inform, and prepare for whatever we wish to accomplish in the community.

A program like the Sant La Fellowship is precisely what we need at this moment. Gepsie has seen the need for her generation, and is ensuring that mine is prepared to take the baton to lead the way.

As I reflect back on these moments, I have come to realize how fortunate and honored I am to have been part of such an amazing team. I came to the fellowship already with a strong belief in the importance of community involvement. The program has only deepened that desire. For that, I am truly grateful.

"Die Empty"

Do yourself and your legacy a BIG favor...DIE EMPTY.

It is a guaranteed fact that, one day, each and every one of us will transition from this life. However, many of us do not remain mindful of this truth. Dominic, one of my coworkers, told me on multiple occasions that he made a personal decision to always reflect on death. Not much because he fears it, on the contrary, because he is grateful for life. He believes that by reflecting on death, he is able to prioritize his life on earth knowing that any day can be his last.

Unfortunately, not everyone reflects on death that way. Most people stay as far away from having any conversation about something that we all know will happen. But it is just a matter of when. That fear is known to be one of the worst human fears, closely followed by the fear of public speaking, the fear of old age, the fear of poverty, and the fear of loss of love. Every effect has its cause. If fear of death is the effect, then the question you should be asking yourself is, "What makes me fear death?" I do not believe we were born fearing something; we develop our fears from our environment, from things and people that we interact with. But the fear of death is global, regardless of our environment. If you live, you die. It is a part of life. We know that one day our time here on earth will run out. The one question I would like to ask everyone, especially you who are reading this book, is this: when your days run out and you are lying on your deathbed, will you reflect on your life and genuinely state with certainty, "Have I served my purpose in this world, and, therefore, I am ready to move on to the next life"?

To answer truthfully, it does not matter where you are and what you are currently doing. The life of every individual matters to their family, the nation and to themselves. That is why we all fear death with an equal measure. So, whether you are a teacher, a farmer, a politician, a doctor, an engineer, or a student, you should ask yourself the same question. Those who say that they are ready to die often feel that they have lived their lives to their full potential. They will die empty, with no more wishes or regrets whatsoever about the way they have spent their days on earth. Their kind of death will resemble that of Jesus. When His time to die came, He was prepared. He was certain that He had fulfilled the scriptures, and He had nothing more left to do in this world. "It is finished" (John 19:30). He died empty.

In order to even dream of experiencing such a blissful death, we must first understand the meaning of life. We have to identify the things that truly matter, and use our energy to work towards them every day of our lives. What matters to me might not necessarily matter to you. But again, that is the beauty of life. Everybody is unique, and we cannot be all the same. The world would be in chaos if life was that way. Imagine a world where everyone was a carpenter. Who would produce food for them to eat? Who would solve disputes among them? Who would provide security to the rest of the people? The essence of our unique abilities is to complement one another. My fellow compatriots in and outside of Haiti are blessed with all kinds of people, with different and special skills and abilities. We must find a way to co-exist and live in peace and appreciation of our neighbors.

We must provide a conducive environment to everyone to do what their heart desires so that when their days run out, they will die having accomplished their goals.

Many failures in life cannot be blamed on external factors. I agree that the pressures and challenges of life can make us drift away from our main goals. Having reflected on this perspective, it is upon each of us to remain steadfast and cling on to our objectives in life no matter what they may be. The goals here are the deepest desires of our hearts. My advice is for you to identify each one of your deepest desires in life and to make achieving them your life's purpose. For a farmer, his greatest desire could be producing an abundance of food year in year out. For a teacher, it could be living to see his or her students grow to be important people who will bring change in Haiti. When these desires are fulfilled, the individuals are filled with great joy. They leave this life with the precious gratification of knowing they have left a mark in the world. A legacy that will be celebrated and remembered for many years to come.

Our daily obligations can often feel like a burden to ourselves. Our responsibilities can trick us into viewing them as hindrances from achieving life goals. On average we hustle to meet deadlines, reach quotas, and strive for promotions, but we allow these jobs to overshadow a sense of true fulfillment. Life can easily turn into a game of mental hopscotch, jumping from one foot to the next trying to make ends meet. Things such as creativity, self-discipline, and innovation are sacrificed by a false idea of priority because many become convinced that life is about prolonging the inevitable. The more appropriate viewpoint is that life should be centered around purpose and the feeling of calm. Once you identify your life's purpose, it should be the center of focus throughout your lifespan. Making the commitment to not only achieve your goals related to this purpose, but share your experiences to the generation to come. This is one way we can make certain that we die empty.

One of the many perks of interning in the director's office at AT&T was the ability to go and listen to live or past speakers during my lunch at the AT&T University internal website. The authors of the book *Multipliers,* Liz Wiseman and leading contributor Greg McKeon, explained that the best leaders make everyone smarter around them. They find a way to inspire their employees or colleagues to give more than 100% instead of just the bare minimum. The authors created an easy map for egocentric managers and micromanagers to follow that would help them move from being diminishers to multipliers.[15]

In my life so far, I have met quite a few multipliers. They vary from mentors to professors, from bosses to coworkers. They have always found the time to pour life lessons into me, and use analogies to give me advice. They are never too far away to give me feedback that helps me develop my leadership skills, and they believe in me when I don't believe in myself. They are always there at the right time, saying the right things to keep me motivated. They do not sugarcoat anything either because they know who I can be when I am focused.

I am saying this to compel you to look around you. Whose skills can you multiply? Is that person a mentee? A little brother or sister? A colleague? A coworker or employee? A son or daughter? I am grateful I had someone like Carline Paul; former mayor of North Miami Beach, Myron Rosner; and former state representative, the late John Patrick Julien, who introduced me to civic engagement in this country, which

---

15 Liz Wiseman, *Multipliers: How the Best Leaders Make Everyone Smarter* (New York: Harper Business, 2017).

helped me take a good look at what was going on in my community. Someone like Professor Pradel Frank and Professor Daphnee Gilles, who helped me in my journey through Miami Dade College and pushed me to be not only a student but also a leader who can focus on solutions when there is a problem.

I'm grateful to have known someone like Mr. Robert Suarez and Ms. Hope Todoroff, who believed in integration instead of exclusion. Since the day I stepped into the office for my Year Up internship, they treated me like one of their own. Mr. Suarez trusted me to do the safety visit with the technicians and trusted my judgment in my reports. He included me in every staff meeting, using any teachable moment to talk to me. He knew it was better to show me how things work instead of telling me. I'm grateful to have someone like Ms. Karen Dunlap in my corner, who gave me a chance in a place where the leading languages are Portuguese and Spanish, yet believed in my ability to compensate for my lack of language skills with hard work and effort. She knew that if I never had an opportunity to prove myself, people would never know how good I could be. And someone like Pastor Gregory Toussaint, who, through his teaching, has made me a better Christian, a better man, a better son, a better husband, and now, a better father.

In one way or another, each one of these leaders contributed to my success; each one taught me a way to better myself. *That* is the power of a stretcher. That is the goal of leading with distinction. True leaders make you see and reach your true potential.

Conclusion

THE COUNTRY WE OUGHT TO DREAM FOR

Alas, we have arrived at our destination point together. It is only proper that we meet united at this intersection as we began this reading journey together., Togetherness is a particularly interesting concept, in that it requires cooperation as well as a collaboration of both sharing and receiving. Indisputably, in true togetherness, all must be willing. I extend my heartfelt congratulations to you, the reader, for your unwavering dedication to travel this path of discovery and revelation with me. Yet, as we stand at this juncture, it is evident that our work, our collective exploration of deeper truths and aspirations, is far from complete. As always, there is much work to be done. But n this closing section, let's probeless as to history. Let's give thanks to the fortitude of promise. I have given you my word that I would share a greater vision of what can be, and I only hope and pray that I have kept my end of the agreement.

It is difficult to believe that I am here at this point. It took me more than six months to think about how I should close the book. I knew I was not done, but I could not place my fingers on the right keys to give the depth of what I wanted to express for posterity. Notably, after my trip to Haiti in February 2017, I could not remove that thought from my mind of "the country we ought to dream for." When the plane landed in Miami, I finally concluded that this is how I wanted to close this part of the journey.

During my most recent trip back to Haiti, I have met so many people. All courageous, inspiring, motivated, and high-spirited, all whose number one objective is help their community. By the same token, I could not ignore what I heard on the news nearly every time I turned on the radio there. Another group of teachers felt compelled to leave to South America in hopes of finding jobs, only to be underpaid.

A group of university students took the dangerous path with the goal of attending school in the U.S. somehow, all while being at risk of becoming shipwrecked before reaching the "Land of the Free and the Home of the Brave." Heard in the background of their journey was one of the most popular songs being sung by almost every young girl and young boy in Haiti, *"Men Madam Papa."* Despite the nature of the song to degrade women and popularize a phenomenon in the country where young girls or young women take refuge in "sugar daddies" to feed them, buy clothes, or pay for tuitions because our society has turned into survival of the fittest, it is still a song of survival.

With a society in such an unstable condition, I feel that the transition from talking to action is long overdue. It is fitting to remind my generation, and the one quickly following us, of the importance of our past and how we came together to achieve what we had achieved.

In order to raise our country up to the version of it in our dreams, we will need to take some serious looks inward and be real with ourselves. This begins with more concentration on issues such as colorism and injustice. Right now, according to a Fox News article, people are dying at an alarming rate because of overcrowded prisons, malnutrition, and infectious diseases.[16] As a matter of fact, most people die without ever having been convicted of a crime. Our penal system is by far the most congested in the world, with an alarming 454% occupancy level, as implied by the Institute for Criminal Policy System. This same research cited that 80% of prisoners were not convicted of a crime. Some inmates wait as long as eight years to see a presiding judge and are all reduced to a state lower than animals, guilty or innocent.

---

16   Fox News report, "Living Hell: Officials Alarmed by Upsurge of Inmates Dying in Haiti Prisons," (Feb 20, 2017). Retrieved from: http://www.foxnews.com/world/2017/02/20/living-hell-officials-alarmed-by-upsurge-inmates-dying-in-haiti-prisons.html

All the deadly prejudices are still alive in the hearts of the masses, and the separation of classes runs amok in our society even as I write this evaluation. It is the bourgeoisie against the poor, the well-spoken French elite looking down upon the Creole-speaking people, and the political charlatans locking down the government to line their own pockets. All the while, the foreigners are running up and down, left and right in the country. To this day, we still have the venom of racism running through our "golden veins," impairing the better angels in our hearts.

An astronomical number of our brothers and sisters still live in ignorance. Affordable and public education, our last and only hope for escaping this vicious cycle, is already degraded and holding on by a thread. Acceptance is what we have become accustomed to, and it has handicapped our royal minds as a consequence. Abject poverty and humiliation do not revolt us anymore. Our cities are left in disarray; our farmers do not farm anymore because no one can afford to buy their goods. And as chaos like this ensures internally, Haiti opens to business for foreign entities.

Haiti cannot open for business to the outside world until it is open to welcoming the diaspora living in all corners of this earth. By welcoming, I mean maintaining new open-door policies that accept the ideas, energy, and political involvement of businessmen, educators, scientists, entrepreneurs, and politicians of Haitians and diasporic Haitians alike.

Our cities are in chaos; our countryside is neglected, with gangs running amok as if they were the rulers of their own anarchic domains. Our communities have turned into open-air jail cells, with kidnapping running rampant and schools shuttering their doors, denying our children the education they so desperately need and deserve. Young boys, who should be our future leaders, are instead being seduced by the allure of power and violence, transforming not into tomorrow's political leaders, but into tomorrow's most feared gang members. I mention these travesties not to paint a bleak picture or appear negative, but to reasonably assess the overall situation we find ourselves in. I am not asking for a quick fix, a feel-good message, or naive hope and a masked change hidden behind a new name with the same face, the same ideology, and spirit of servitude towards the **WHITE MASTERS**.

In the midst of the turmoil that plagues our beloved Haiti, I cannot help but feel that we have failed the very ancestors who fought so valiantly for our freedom. The dreams they held dear, the visions they had for our nation, have devolved into haunting nightmares that plague our collective consciousness. Yet, despite the seemingly insurmountable challenges that face us, this generation holds within its grasp the potential to ignite a new revolution – a rebirth of a Haiti that reimagines its future unfettered by the shackles of its tumultuous past.

At the dawn of our fight for freedom, it was the words of Toussaint Louverture that served as the beacon of hope, as well as the precursor to our eventual triumph. As I close this chapter, we must not forget the unwavering resolve of Jean-Jacques Dessalines, whose tenacity and fierce determination ultimately delivered us from the clutches of colonialism. In his own words, Dessalines declared, "I only want to keep the brave with me. Let those who want to become French slaves again leave the fort. On the contrary, let those who want to die as free men line up around me. Will black people, whose fathers are in Africa, have nothing?"

Today, as we stand at the crossroads of history, we are faced with a choice – to be the brave that Dessalines spoke of, to stand united in our quest for a renewed Haiti. Just as the farmers at the Canal pressed on, undeterred by external threats, so too must we forge ahead, guided by the same indomitable spirit that has defined our people for centuries.

And so, I call upon each and every one of us, the sons and daughters of Haiti, to return to our roots, embrace our heritage, and join hands with our brothers and sisters on the home front. Together, we can rebuild the Haiti that we all hold dear, a nation that is steeped in the rich legacy of our ancestors, who gave their sweat and blood for the cause of freedom.

Let us draw inspiration from our storied past, from the unity that was our ancestors' guiding principle. For it was their collective strength, their unwavering resolve to live free or die, that carved out our place in history as the first black independent nation, as the second country in the Western Hemisphere to claim independence, and as the sole victors of a successful slave rebellion. Our history is our greatest teacher, and it is time for us to heed its lessons to embrace the motto that carried our ancestors to victory: "Through Unity Comes Strength." It is with that same resolution that we must embrace and welcome each and every Haitian and Haitian descendant living outside the country. The call they gave yesterday still stands today; it is still ringing in our ears, imploring us to wake from our slumber because the survival of the nation depends on it.

We will succeed if we can draw our strength from their inspiration, if we can purge hatred, reject political selfishness, open Haiti to its sons and daughters, remove the mentality of *"konstitisyon se papye, bayonet se fè,"* (the constitution is paper, the bayonet is iron) and turn towards a system of law, and teach our civilians to be law-abiding citizens. To restore true love for our neighbors, the mulattos and the peasants, the rich and the poor.

Let the educated see the uneducated as their brothers, fund better schools, and pay teachers to educate them. Let the rich see the poor as their neighbors and pay them better wages. Let the poor see the rich as those who share the same Dessalinian blood, protect them and not let ourselves be used as pawns to drive the very people the country needs to survive away from their homes. Let the political leaders see the next generation as the next best hope for Haiti, not as a threat to be destroyed in order to protect their seat in power.

Together, and only together, can we see the Haiti our forefathers had intended for us. Together, and only together, can Haiti regain its proper place among the great nations once more. Together, and only together, can ALL OF US prosper again. Together, and only together, can we cry in the same optimistic voice as the precursor of our independence. We might not all make it to the Promised Land, but "our roots are deep and numerous," and I am confident that our sons and daughters shall see it so one day.

It is my hope, my aspiration, and my burning conviction that the wall our enemies have built to divide us will come down through our unity — and our love of our beloved Haiti.

ACKNOWLEDGMENTS

It takes a village to raise a kid well. This accomplishment was no different. I literally had an army of family, friends, and strangers helping make this a reality. I owe a debt of gratitude to Grace Mbuyi. It was just a reference from a coworker; we talked briefly via text and scheduled a face-to-face meeting. Little did I know that conversation around a table in a bookstore in Brickell would lead to a friend who made it her duty to make the book the best it can be. It has been quite an adventure since that day we met.

A special thank you to Dominic Saintil. I could have written a book, but not one that will leave an indelible memory in people's minds. His insight, personal feedback, and most importantly his realist view of the world has pushed me to write something real with no sugarcoating. He is a good friend, a true friend. For that I thank him.

What good is a memoir if you cannot rely on the family who was right there with you in those moments? From the start of the book, I knew that I would need to rely heavily on my parents and siblings to share some of their memories with me when I was younger or go back even before I was born to understand a historical event or cultural connection with some issues. Samuella Guillaume and my mother led the charge in making sure I had all my questions answered. So many of them gave me countless hours of their precious time. Without their insights and help, I would not be able to even start this book. There are various other people who have helped as well.

A special thank you to Christina Drill for assisting me in editing this new edition of my first-ever book. Their dedication to excellence and desire to print the best book possible was invaluable. I want to express my thanks to Mr. Gerald Chertavian for the foreword to the book.

ACKNOWLEDGMENTS

Finally, last but certainly never least, is my wife, my friend, and my partner in this endeavor, Elpidia, who has been my cornerstone and my greatest supporter. Unconditional support is something we many times take for granted. In all, thank you, Elpidia, for being my biggest fan.

Over the past seven years, our family has grown and evolved in the most beautiful way. The addition of Dawid and Daud has brought even more joy and fulfillment to our lives. All three of our children, Dahveed, Dawid, and Daud, have made me a better father. I look forward to coming home every day, knowing that I will be greeted in the best way possible by not just one, but all three, of these incredible little humans. The love and happiness they bring to my life is immeasurable, and I am grateful for them each and every day.

Made in the USA
Columbia, SC
13 March 2024